THE DANCE OF THE PILGRIM

THE DANCE OF THE PILGRIM

A Christian Style of Life for Today

by

JOHN DAVID MAGUIRE

ASSOCIATION PRESS

NEW YORK

THE DANCE OF THE PILGRIM

Copyright © 1967 by
National Board of Young Men's Christian Associations
Association Press, 291 Broadway, New York, N.Y. 10007

Acknowledgement is hereby made of quotations cited in this book from the following sources:

From *An American Dream* by Norman Mailer. Copyright © 1964, 1965 by Norman Mailer and used with permission of the publishers, The Dial Press, Inc.

From *The Moviegoer* by Walker Percy and *The Plague* by Albert Camus, used with permission of Alfred A. Knopf, Inc.

From *A Portrait of the Artist as a Young Man* by James Joyce. Copyright 1916 by B. W. Huebsch, Inc., 1944 by Nora Joyce. Reprinted by permission of The Viking Press, Inc.

From *Other Voices, Other Rooms,* by Truman Capote, used with permission of the publishers, Random House, Inc.

From *The Ballad of the Sad Café*, by Carson McCullers, used with permission of the publishers, Houghton Mifflin Co.

From *A Generous Man,* by Reynolds Price, used with permission of the publishers, Athaneum Publishers.

Publisher's stock number: 1643 hardcover;

1647P paperbound

Library of Congress catalog card number: 67-14587

Printed in the United States of America

Preface

At the publication of *My Hope for America*, President Johnson's hurried-up campaign collection of previous speeches, he emphatically declared: "I have actually spoken every word in this book." Unlike President Johnson, I have not only spoken virtually every word in this volume but have written each word as well!

This little book originated as a set of lectures. All five of them were delivered together only once, at the 73rd Annual Northfield, Massachusetts, Conference For Girls, June 17–23, 1966. However, parts of the text were used in lectures at Brown University, at Rice University, and at the annual New England Student Christian Movement Conference at Camp O–At–Ka, Maine. In every instance I was asked to sketch an appropriate and viable style of life for Christians in the contemporary world, indicating that mysterious interaction between belief and practice, thinking and doing, "faith and morals," theology and ethics. This I sought to do. I have thoroughly reworked those lectures into the text you have here.

I must pay special tribute and acknowledge a special debt to my great former teacher, Professor Robert L. Calhoun, of Yale. Chapters 3 and 4 draw most heavily from his work. Indeed the pattern of organization as well as much of the substance of these chapters reflects portions of his course in Systematic Theology given at the Yale Divinity School during the late fifties, in which I was privileged to serve as his assistant.

I stress throughout this volume the highly improvisatory character of Christian existence as well as its demand for a communal context. My deepest gratitude goes to those many who have generously and freely borne with me "on the way" and have taught me what I know about "the form of faithful living."

John David Maguire

Contents

FOR MY DAUGHTERS
KELLY, CATHERINE, MARY ELIZABETH

I

Coping with Chaos

"The flood of mortal ills prevailing
This world with devils filled
The grinning prince of darkness grim
Earthly powers that kill."

These snatches from Luther's *Ein Feste Burg* surely have their counterpart in the headlines of any week's newspapers any year of our lives: "Arthritis Is Killer and Crippler, says National Institute," "Tornadoes Spin Death and Destruction in Midwest," "Wife Hacks Husband To Death, Watches Him Die," "Plane Crashes with 54 Aboard," "Johnson Warns That Loss of South Vietnam Is Loss of Southeast Asia," "Another City Woman Raped," "Tri-State Power Failure: the Lights Go Out."

This kind of demon-filled world—full of poor people who are miserable, sick people who are hurt and frightened, and the dead who are nothing—provokes a partial paralysis in some people over life's meaninglessness; self-accusing, self-crippling guilt in many; and obsessions with death itself in others.

Some can't move without guidelines. Many wake up to the fact that even before they were conscious they contributed somehow to the world's misery, and that awakening ravages them with guilt. Others freeze the moment they become aware that *they* will die. So said Paul Tillich.* And he was right. Warped or diseased cocoons produce maimed butterflies.

This kind of world has brought forth a distinctive literature in America—the literature of Ellison, Styron, Bowles, Bellow, Mailer, Roth, Purdy, Hawkes, and Burroughs (to name its major practitioners). Their literature shares some convictions about our life. My colleague at Wesleyan, Professor Ihab Hassan, has neatly characterized these convictions. In the vision of these current novelists, he writes,

1. Chance and absurdity rule human actions. What the philosophers call "reality" is really chaos. There are no real causes, only twitches and spasms, ludicrous and grinding.

2. There are no accepted norms—of feeling

---

* The sources of this reference and others on succeeding pages are listed under References at the back of the book.

or conduct—to which a man may appeal. There is no general standard for thought or for action to which one may refer unfailingly.

3. To live is to be at odds—with environment, with others, with oneself—and so always to be somehow an alien, a misfit. Others aren't aids and comforts, but others are the enemy.

4. *The* characteristic of life, of personal existence, is ambiguity. Human motives are forever mixed; irony and contradiction prevail. No thought or action is ever pure. Blameless purity is an impossibility, but pure pusillanimity is probably also ruled out. Free and yet a slave, actor yet acted upon; everything is mixed. And one who is completely neutralized is in danger of becoming neuter.

5. A man can't know much. Limitation and relativism, tininess and partiality are the major marks of our manhood.

That is the substance of an understanding of our situation shared by our best novelists. The heroes and antiheroes in their novels adopt a certain style or "way of life" in their efforts to cope with existence, a style which increasingly commends itself to those who view the world their way. What has moved them to this position?

11

Nearly fifty years ago Sigmund Freud provided an analysis which may contribute to an explanation. He saw the ego wrestling with the imperious, urgent demands of the self, the world with its necessary conventions, and a stern, reproving, Father-Judge. Instructed by Freud's account, the generation just before us, aping the primal brother band, took care of God, the cosmic version of the Judging Father. Culturally speaking, they either killed him so that he's dead and gone forever, or, letting him live, cut his larynx so he no longer speaks or sings, or robbed him of all agency and vitality so that he remains confined to Heaven, an ineffectual, unitary blob.

That is what has happened to God in our generation. Or so some of our most sensitive seers contend.

"What about the world—firm, solid nature?" you may ask. "Surely it remains something to trust and hang on to." Yet when we study nature we discover *dis*order, not harmony or classical causality. The very terminology through which we are now taught to order our thinking about nature bespeaks fragmentation: radio-active disintegration, transmutation, indeterminacy, fission. The symmetries, the simple laws have all disappeared. The deeper we descend into the depths of nature—through, say, particle physics—the more we discover a vast sea of chaotic disorder in which these particles continually change and rearrange, a whole sea of "virtual" particles that, as Gerald Holton has said, for small intervals of time disobey all the classical laws. If we suspect that our scientific explanations approximate ever closer "things as they are," then nature too is increasingly understood as utterly chaotic.

God seems dead, nature chaotic. What about the self, man's last stronghold? Instead of seeking out the vital and the stimulating, we selves have developed a passion for safety and security, retreating from the world but not dangerously deep within ourselves. Walker Percy has one self-protecting character in his novel, *The Moviegoer,* protest: "Anyone but an idiot knows this is a good life and anyone but a scoundrel can lead it." Later he has her comment a little more pensively: "I have a little hubby whom I see off in the morning, I have lunch with the girls, I get tight about twice a month at parties and flirt. I wear my little diaphragm and raise my two lovely boys and worry for the next twenty years whether they will make Princeton." I judge that this self-occupied emptiness is a special kind of hell and is symbolic of the self's plight.

Given that this is our situation, at least as it appears in many modern novels and as it seems to many nonliterateurs, let's analyze three fundamental ways or primal patterns in terms of which we try to cope in this kind of darkened world. I now intend to pull apart three life styles. In labeling these ways "styles," I purposely mean to draw your attention to style as literary critics, such as Richard Poirier, refer to it.

Style, in their understanding, is a complex unity. Every piece of literature exemplifies it. It distinguishes pieces of literature from each other. For purposes of analysis, style can be broken up into parts—form and content, shape and substance—but before and after such artificial analyses, style is one whole, complex thing.

So understood, style in literature is a parable of personal existence.

Just as literary style is made up of shape *and* substance, so a "life-style" is composed of beliefs and actions. It too is a complex unity. Life-style is important, for one's "self" is determined by the "style" to which one is committed. We *are* committed to styles. Some are adopted for the sake of expressing our personal depths, our "substance," most completely. Others are adopted in order to conceal our depths, especially the seamier elements.

We choose our styles in part, and in part they seem simply to develop. But insofar as we choose them we are making a fundamental decision—"opting," as the psychologists say, "for a distinctive model of selfhood." So though complex unities, we live with *some* interplay between belief and action whether we are *conscious* of it or not, and that interplay—its shape and substance—constitutes our style.

The analogy between literary works and personal existence goes even further, for when we *do* become conscious of styles—life-styles —the choice between them is not unlike judgments about works of art. We have to weigh many factors—line, pattern, hue—and then evaluate. We could even say that artistic evaluation is a paradigm of moral decision.

It is with this understanding of life-style, then, that we are working. And my thesis about those three that we are examining now is that, while none of them constitutes *the*

Christian way, each contains partial aspects of that style and each springs from fundamental human powers or faculties that must not be denied.

The Way of the Aesthete, Active or Passive

Whenever you conclude that Life, the Country of the City of Man, is not only nasty, brutish, and short but also dissolving and dying in the darkness, you might try to transcend it by soaring into Another Country, the timeless City of Art where there is pure light and life. When your country and world is "black and blind as a bat," when flesh is wordless, mindless, nonsensical, when everything is going under, you might try to strive with your imagination—that "virgin womb where the word is made flesh"—to create "out of the sluggish matter of the earth a new soaring impalpable imperishable being." Leave the daily bread and common wine unattended and of course they'll rot, but let the artist—the high priest of the eternal imagination—rework them in words or pigments and they can be "transmuted into the radiant body of everlasting life." One thinks immediately of James Joyce's *A Portrait of the*

16

Artist as a Young Man, from which I've been quoting. We think of Joyce's young artist, Stephen Daedalus, of Joyce's whole career, and of the efforts of dancers like Merce Cunningham and writers like John Updike and Reynolds Price in our generation. They represent the actively aesthetic way of coping with ourselves and the world.

This way is especially attractive in our time when everything has become fragmented, when all the pieces of existence have been rendered equally meaningless. In that situation any bit or piece of word, language, or visual detail is as worthy of being worked with or put together as any other. "Constantly to express," declares young Stephen, "to press out again from the gross earth, from sound and shape and color which are the prison gates of our soul, an image of beauty we have come to understand—that is art." Expression is everything. It is the way. (That, of course, is why we went through that period in art instruction when there was virtually no concern with the content of what the student painted or sculpted. The whole emphasis focused on the act of creativity itself.) The act of constructing pieces into something, expressing, becomes the

17

important thing. The unfolding form, not so much the content, interests the active aesthete, for all content, by itself shapeless, is otherwise trivial. Thus we identify artists, especially contemporary ones, by the form(s) that they adopt in expressing or giving shape to their experience.

This aesthetic way of coping with the self and the world is also inviting when all the ground rules, cosmic or otherwise, have vanished. This frees us to play, to make up our rules as we go along. The only requisite is that, once posited, these rules be observed for some period of time in order to keep the game the game.

This kind of aesthetic way addresses itself especially to that first dimension of darkness which Tillich noted, namely, meaninglessness. Begin whistling, skipping, playing. Whistle a tune (it gives a form to the moment). Do something (it's bound to have a shape). Move (movement makes a path or pattern). And *after* you've done something expressive, you may look back and *recognize* a form in it or discover some meaning. Many of us do far more. We literally learn to practice some art— music, painting, writing, dancing—with such passion and devotion that for a long time our art gives meaning to our lives.

This aesthetic way, however, is adopted by hordes of us who are not practicing artists at all. We might be called passive aesthetes. All of us who, consciously or not, seek to escape, to transcend our existence by dreaming of what we'd like to own, or become; who fill our time with fantasies; who seek new, always thrilling situations; who love the zany, the eccentric, the bizarre; whose lives have become simply a string of episodic excitations, sensual or dreamy. Sören Kierkegaard declared that all of us who court the romantic, horde and take pleasure in our own melancholy, whose life itself becomes the sole shape or form which we fill with experience, practice the aesthetic way. Homosexuals and drug-users often describe drifting into this dreamy world in the search for something richer, more vivid, something different. Though neither homosexuals nor dope-users, all of us who exhibit the kinds of symptoms I've suggested pursue second-hand or passive aestheticism. The housewife who fills her mind, while doing the week's chores, with thoughts of the Saturday night party at which she'll appear in a smashing op-art dress copied right out of the latest *Vogue*. The male student, soothed by mood music, curled up alone, urgently perusing *Playboy*. The young father whose commuter trip home is alternately filled with dreams of a still bigger boat or of some romantic conquest he's just seen negotiated in the movies by Paul Newman. These people—and aren't we often like them? —are the passive, second-hand aesthetes.

I say "second-hand" because we try to transcend our threatening world, not by expressing, shaping, or creating ourselves, but by exploiting someone else's expressiveness—escaping into the novelist's world, not writing our own novel; watching television, not perceiving the world and painting it; going to dances rather than mastering the dance. We don't really transcend through expression. We escape by using materials that other people have provided for us. We don't create; we use. Passive aestheticism is derivative existence.

Whether actively or passively, whether authentic or derivative, the aesthetic way has great strengths. It involves a special kind of responsibility—that of giving self and world whatever shape they'll have. At its best it makes imagination paramount. It stresses a special kind of action—the act of expression. It elicits and requires play. It requires that the mind work, not dully, but with flair.

But the way of the aesthete also has weaknesses. It is dedicated to art, not life. It seeks to transcend the world, to soar above it—not to remain in the world, to burrow into it—and that may bring disaster as it did to Daedalus and to Icarus, who flew too near the sun. The airy City of Art is free but thin. It lacks earth, it lacks actuality. Indeed, having decided to go in fantasy where I cannot go in fact, I may eventually lose the ability to distinguish between envisaging and enacting. And I am in danger when dreams, as fundamental as they are, have become more real than facts. And again, this aesthetic life can be an utterly *self*-centered existence where *my* expressiveness, *my* finding *my* form is all that matters.

In the chaos every man seeks to establish some control. The aesthete does it by abstracting, transcending the chaos of the actual world to a new world of his making. But even if one could ultimately flee *away* from darkness into light, would this not be empty escaping? And suppose, *mirabile dictu,* he should make it, alone, wouldn't he be the loneliest fellow in his new world? "Can anyone live apart in happy oblivion?" asks Rambert in *The Plague*, by Albert Camus.

Such is the first style I see many of us adopting as we cope with existence.

The primitive pattern is that of Odyssey, the mask is an o-so-sad smile, and the archetypal or symbolic figure is Adam's third son, Seth, the builder who created sons for earth.

The Way of The Victim

A second basic style for coping with the self and the world in darkness is for the self to absorb the assaults of the world, to yield itself to the world as victim. Many critics are convinced that Christianity bids believers to adopt this response. Ernst Troeltsch urged that while Calvinism mastered the world, his beloved Lutheranism endured the world in suffering, pain, and martyrdom. Dietrich Bonhoeffer calls us to "suffer with God at the hands of a godless world," and one of his principal interpreters, Professor William Hamilton, calls all of us—men as well as women—to discover "the female dimension" in our ethical experience, which he associates with passivity, receptivity, the capacity to absorb, to take drudgery and dullness.

Instead of fretting with Margaret Mead over fathers increasingly doing traditionally women's work, Hamilton welcomes it, for in doing it men are actually participating in the feminine.

There is something very profound here, about living a resignation that redeems, receiving rather than always attacking, learning not always to be active, strangely finding joy in suffering. It also has its bizarre forms: some homosexuals use the same terms to explain their commitments—the passion for passivity, to suffer, to take another, to take the world, into oneself, to find a joy in being hurt.

The way of the victim begins with silence—feeling things, absorbing insults, witnessing woes—and not talking or striking back. As one absorbs the world, however, that expanding ingested part becomes an ever greater barrier between oneself and the rest of the world. It becomes a harder and harder fight to stay in *that* world, and so the victim often goes limp, allowing himself to be carried along like a ping-pong ball down a mountain stream—a resistanceless course that leads often to neurosis and insanity. He hasn't fled into unreality; he has simply let himself be carried there.

And once committed to absorbing the world —which is bound *eventually* to bring one's death (through drowning, suffocation, or glut) —one may find enroute, before coming to his natural end, something calling one prematurely to death. And so the correlation between the way of the victim and suicide.

Suicide is a lonely landscape [cries the hero of a current Norman Mailer novel] with the pale light of a dream, and there are lyric tunes—like a pure quartet—which sound in the depth . . . In my forty-fourth year I began to hear them, tuning up. And then that night the Moon played the tune —that platinum lady with her silver light—calling musically, "Come to me, come now, don't wait. End your suffering now." And I felt my foot go over the balustrade.

The way of the victim has special attraction, now that, culturally speaking, God is dead, in resolving that second dimension of our darkness that Tillich noted, namely, the continuing burden of guilt. Strangely enough, guilt still haunts many of us even in a godless world. And this is a way of working it out, expiating. I have a colleague who once told me that he would like every Saturday night to take off his shirt, lean against the wall, and let everybody that he had harmed that week come by, pick up a bull whip, and take out a fair number of lashes. "Of course I'd be a bloody mess every Saturday night," he said, "but at least I would have paid up all the debts every week. I wouldn't be spiritually, morally, always in debt."

Many of us elect the way of the victim, some authentically, suffering in silence, letting ourselves be used, leading an inner life outsiders don't see. Others of us elect it inauthentically, masochistically, homosexually, neurotically, suicidally. Most of us stand somewhere between: all of us who need to fail and do; all of us who overextend ourselves in order to wound and defeat ourselves; all of us who court destructive danger; all of us who hurl ourselves without qualification into ambiguous or questionable causes, secretly hoping we'll get hurt and settle our debt to someone; all of us who are like the noble lady who said, "My pleasure in the bitter dislike of my own imperfection is actually the most secret and perilous hiding-place of my pride." We all take the way of the victim.

Though we don't actually commit suicide, we identify ourselves with pathetic heroines like William Styron's Peyton Loftis in *Lie Down In Darkness,* whose prayer on the way to her self-destruction can be paraphrased: "God, give me my Daddy back; Daddy, give me my God back, for somewhere I've lost my way." We reject authors and preachers who point a way as if they were peddlers of quack nostrums. We secretly delight in having no way. We want no way. Give us the lostness. We long to be "poor little lambs" forever.

This way has great strengths. It knows that there is no authentic experience without suffering. It cultivates that special sensitivity to hurt, to all violated life. It makes tender feeling paramount. It *can* short-circuit the flow of public evil by arresting it within oneself and by refusing to pass it on. It exalts being acted upon. It makes *feeling* preëminent.

But the way of the victim has crippling weaknesess. Since existence is rhythmic it has too *little* place for act and expression. It makes suffering, an inescapable component of experience, the *end* of experience. One cannot finally absorb the world, take the whole "prickly-wrapped thing" into oneself. And insofar as guilt is the motivation for choosing this way, it is doomed; for if infidelity to others and oneself and the violation of nature produced the guilt, only *their* forgiveness releases. What if they are on the other side of the country, or the other side of the world? What if they are now dead?

Like the aesthete, the victim seeks control—but by absorbing, taking it all in, rather than by transcending. Yet the way of the victim fills without fulfilling.

Such is the second style many of us adopt. Its primitive pattern is the ritual *agon,* the offering of the lamb to be killed. Its mask is the grimace, and the archetypal or symbolic figure is Adam's second son, Abel, who was slain by his brother.

The Way of The Aggressor

"There are times," Norman Cohn observes of the eleventh century, "when people living in a state of chronic frustration and anxiety find that sense of anxious impotence and envy suddenly discharged into a frantic urge to kill, to smite the ungodly, to blaze a new world into being with blood."

The mass killers—Charles Starkweather, Richard Speck, Charles Whitman—are the extreme representatives of the aggressor. They actualize that way. And there is undeniably mounting in our time an attraction to this third way, which wearies of laying down one's life, being beat upon, and silently suffering. It views the darkness as malevolent and sees the taking of other life—sometimes actually, always symbolically—as the only way of maintaining one's own life.

The way of the aggressor may have humble origins. It may begin simply as rebellion—against everything for which the Father is the symbol: the past, tradition, coercive authority, religion, the Church. But it rapidly generalizes until a kind of credo, sketched by Arthur McGill, is born: "The supreme exhibition of power [which the aggressor seeks] is to be able to kill another, to be able to deprive another of life in order to enhance or secure my own."

A great part of Norman Mailer's early work spoke for this way. Just a few years ago, in *Advertisements For Myself,* he asserted that his next novel would be a "dissection of the extreme, the obscene and the unsayable," a tale of heroic villains, passionate lovers, orgy-masters, perverts and murderers raising "moral complexities more interesting than we've gotten into yet." That Big Novel has yet to appear, but an earnest of it, a portent, has. In this work, *An American Dream,* the hero, with an obviously erotic satisfaction, manages to strangle his estranged heiress wife by the end of the first chapter!

I felt my arm tightening about her neck. My eyes were closed. I had the mental image that I was pushing with my shoulder against an enormous door which would give inch by inch to the effort. Spasms of black-biled lust exploded within me. *Crack* I choked her hard and *crack* the door flew open and *crack* tore the wire in her throat and I was through the door. I was weary with the most honorable fatigue and my flesh seemed new. I had not felt so nice since I was twelve. And there was Deborah dead beside me on the flowered carpet of the floor, and there was no question of that: She was dead, indeed she was dead.

Were this literature simply the old psychic safety-valve, designed for us second-handers to ventilate aggression and continue our rather bland outer lives, we might dismiss it. But for many it functions as *credo*. Many homosexuals understand their role as aggressors, not vic-

tims, as killers, not lovers. Many business-
men, euphemistically labeled "entrepreneurial
types," find justification in this gospel of the
necessary kill. Somebody has to lose so that
they can win; somebody's got to remain poor
so that we can be rich. There is something increasingly fascinating about scalding violence,
mutilating outrages, assassination. This "killing of another" has an odd exhilaration within
it. It is never unsexual. It offers the promise of
vast relief.

And murder, of course, can take many
forms short of outright killing. Many of us do
it, as Carson McCullers noted, by our insis-
tence that we be lovers, never beloved.

The fact that love is a joint experience does not
mean that it is a similar experience to the two
people involved. The lover and the beloved come
from different countries. The lover can be man,
woman, child, any human creature on this earth
. . . and the beloved [is usually] only a stimulus
for all that stored up love within the lover. The
lover therefore determines the value and quality
of any love . . . And it is for this reason that most
of us insist on loving rather than being loved. In a
deep secret way the state of being beloved is in-
tolerable to many.

Always having to be on top, always on the attack, maintaining our being only by beating another. Castrating authorities, crippling adversaries.

The way of the aggressor wrestles with the third dimension of our darkness which Tillich noted—our being stalked by death. Unlike the tepid who live in fear that the bomb *might* fall, the aggressor knows that some bomb is going to fall sometime. Old dirty death will intercept one too soon. The only way to preserve one's life is to become a death dealer oneself, to beat back death's assaults by actively identifying with it, to do others in before they—the agents of death—do you in. Thus the aggressor seeks to cope with death by one-upping it.

For all its symbolic and actual brutality, the way of the aggressor has some strengths. In an age that delights in the derivative, relishes the second-hand, and lives in the passive voice, this way demands doing, being there, having the experience, existing in the active voice. It *can* take positive forms—attacking poverty, assaulting illiteracy, and assisting the underdeveloped. There is something positive about being there and doing and not settling for reports in newspapers and novels. There is exhilaration in plunging in.

Yet the version of this way one most frequently sees involves pitting oneself against all others. For the aggressor, control in the dark chaos is not gained by transcendence (as with the aesthete), nor by painful absorbing (as with the victim), but by domination. Domination alone, it insists, impresses men. The leader rules by the fear that others feel for his force. Power and domination alone provide control.

Narcissism and self-hate are often the root of this way. My monumental self-love may drive me to try to extend myself—my will, my way—into and over others even if I destroy them in the process. The martinet father mesmerizing his children, the dictatorial boss tyrannizing his employees may be narcissistic aggressors. Or their assaults may grow out of a self-hatred which drives them to destroy all those who, like human mirrors, remind them of themselves. The compulsion to see *another's* face when mortally wounded is often the desire to extend and see oneself.

The man who must always be moving, wrestling, winning, is finally not free. If the good life also includes bliss and peace and these come only in repose, the aggressor cannot have them. They always elude him.

Thus we have the third principal response to our "dark situation"—the way of answering "the-other-which-threatens" with aggression. The primitive pattern is gladiatorial combat. The mask is a leer, and the archetypal figure is Adam's first son, Cain, who rose up and slew his brother.

Now, to summarize this first chapter: Whatever one believes metaphysically or ontologically, *culturally* speaking God is dead, silent, or impotent. The heavenly lights have gone out. The world—nature and society, cosmos and man—threatens the self, principally in the guise of meaninglessness, guilt, or death. We respond to this dangerous darkness primarily as aesthetes, victims, or aggressors. We seek to control our chaos by transcending it, absorbing it, or plunging into it to kill, assaulting it into submission. None of us is simply one of these types. But we probably do tend to respond dominantly or habitually in one of these styles, although we possess the others recessively or latently and on occasion exhibit them. We are sometimes one, then another.

The first way stresses expressiveness and

puts its premium on perception and imagination. The second way stresses feeling and puts its premium on emotions and sensitivity. The third way stresses doing and puts its premium on the will, and the agencies of action.

We noted weaknesses in each of these styles, or primal patterns. But if there is to be another, superior, style, it must surely include the strengths of these fundamental ways. And if it is to be truly fulfilling, it must engage these powers of the self that are the basis for the fundamentally human responses we've examined.

Revelation is the religious name for the power that takes these styles and transfigures them. The classical Christian contention has been that this power—revelation—*does* make contact with our gropings, addressing and fulfilling these faculties which compose the self. It transfigures these styles, not by denying their humanity and converting them into a transhuman (which would be an antihuman), alien style, but by elevating and amplifying their strengths while muting their weaknesses. We have the world with us—"the flood of mortal ills prevailing, the prince of darkness, powers that kill." Yet, says the Christian Gospel, having all this, we have heaven too. It is this claim and its implications which we must explore in the second chapter.

II

Something Present
Often Missed

John Calvin would have been displeased by the sequence adopted in this volume. "Nearly all the wisdom we possess," he declared, "consists of two parts: the knowledge of God and of ourselves . . . And the proper order requires us to discuss *God* first and then proceed to treat ourselves . . . since no man ever achieves a clear knowledge of himself unless he has first looked upon God's face and *then* descends from contemplating Him to scrutinize himself."

We have reversed Calvin's sequence, having analyzed our situation in immanent cultural terms in the first chapter. However, Calvin conceded that even if one proceeds wrongly—as, in his terms, we've done—"no one can look upon himself without immediately having his thoughts turned to the contemplation of God". . . for "seeing our own ignorance, vanity, poverty, infirmity, and—what is more—depravity and corruption, we recognize that the true light of wisdom, sound virtue, full abundance of every good, and purity of righteousness rest in the Lord alone . . . and to this extent we are prompted by our own ills to contemplate the good things of God . . . Accordingly contemplating ourselves may not only arouse us to *seek* God, but actually leads us by the hand to find him."

Let's see if Calvin is right. We began with ourselves. But the self, we rapidly discovered, is "a many-sided thing." In his autobiography, the late Professor Arthur Schlesinger, Sr., noted: "I came to realize that human situations seldom lend themselves to categorical treatment; that the analysis of the human problem may well yield multiple answers; indeed that this is the normal characteristic of the human process."

The self is surely one of these "situations" that cannot be unraveled by one category. Indeed social psychologists now refer to us as "situations," stressing the confluence of the many forces within us and the layers of reaction that result. Philosophers call the self a "pre-categoreal" or "trans-categoreal, multi-modal reality"—their own rather abstruse way of underlining the same point: we have many abilities, we exercise many powers, and we are not exhausted or explained by the analysis of any or all of them. We require many categories for our understanding and often yield multiple answers to questions addressed to us.

Fully aware of this many-sidedness of selfhood, we nevertheless perceived certain of our powers when we examined some characteristic human responses to existence—transcending, indeed fleeing, absorbing, or plunging into it. The mind, especially in its moments of imagination, seems the primary human power for "the aesthetic way," at least that of the abstractionist or formalist. The emotions, or feelings, especially in almost suffering sensitivity, seem the ground for "the way of the victim." The will—that part of us that decides and acts, especially going forth in action—is at the root of "the way of the aggressor."

Any one of these ways pursued exclusively is doomed to inadequacy, if only by virtue of its partiality. And the hum and throb of the parts of the self from which they spring testify to the incompleteness of these parts or powers—their reaching out for something not yet present to them.

Our *minds* long for an understanding whose vague shape and contours we can imagine, but do not possess. Our *emotions* need reordering, for we often find ourselves "hating that which we would ordinarily love and admiring all which we would usually despise," and this, suggests Norman Mailer, "may be the cause beneath other causes for our sickness and our death." We are drowning in guilt. Our *wills* either spastically galvanize themselves in a series of relatively uncontrolled compulsive actions or remain impotent in the face of things that we should do but seemingly can not. "Man is fallen," insisted Augustine, "and the consequences are *ignorantia, concupiscentia, impotentia*"—ignorance, lust, impotence.

Who can say that any one of these powers or faculties is the key to the others? That the solving of one of these problems would automatically unravel the riddle of the others?

If there is to be any fulfillment of the faculties, any antidote to these confusions, it must surely address itself to all of them at once. If such a surpassing actuality as the self is to be fulfilled, it must be by another "pre-categoreal, trans-categoreal" surpassing actuality. "The human problem demands multiple answers indeed." Quintus Symmachus, the old Roman, was right: "The heart of so great a mystery cannot ever be reached by following one road only."

The Many Modes of Revelation

Christianity and Judaism have always testified that revelation, like the self, is one of these surpassing realities which has many parts. It produces *perception* for blind minds, illumining benighted imaginations. It grants *pardon* for, and makes *demands* upon, misdirected emotions now fixed on perversities. It generates *power* for the impotent, and ability for restraint in the aggressor.

It is most significant, I think, that in roughly corresponding fashion the three main Biblical images for revelation are: "light in darkness" (stressing revelation's address to the mind), "forgiveness of sin" (which is addressed to the emotions) and "power from the Spirit" (which clearly addresses itself to the will).

Another ostensibly different pattern can be found in the structure of our English language, and in the structure of all the languages that are members of our same language family. All of them are divided into moods: the indicative, the imperative, and the subjunctive.

These two disparate observations—one from Scripture, the other from the nature of language—when taken together, provide a natural pattern for our examination of revelation. When revelation comes primarily as perception, it comes in the indicative mood. When revelation comes primarily as pardon, it comes, strangely enough, in the imperative. And when revelation comes primarily as power, its initial address is in the subjunctive.

Clearly, I am adopting a heavily schematic device that, like all schematizations of realities that resist neat categorization, is somewhat misleading. Forgiveness and pardon, for example, often come in the indicative as well as the imperative mood. One might say that *each* human power is addressed by God in *all* the major moods. Talking about revelation in this comprehensive fashion, however, would be almost impossible—"multi-modality" to the point of unspeakable complexity! Treat these pairings, then, as suggestive rather than exhaustive. They are reports of primary ways in which revelation has in fact confronted men.

The aesthetic way, we noted, is marked by

a relentless reaching out into the empyrean for something imagined but not possessed. The artistic world of this striving, transcending way suffers from a deficiency of actuality. Revelation repeatedly meets this kind of striving as imaged flesh. It encounters the hungry mind, the straining imagination, as Fact. It addresses us in the *indicative* mood. "This is it." "I am He." "And when the eyes are opened," says Calvin, "we see that, like the sun, the Word has been shining all along, but of no benefit to us because we had been blind. When the Spirit penetrates into our minds, our eyes are opened, our blindness healed, and at last we see."

Light breaks forth on the aesthete as embodied declaration, and this fact feeds the hungry mind. This fleshly image fulfills the imagination with its concrete presence. This is the fulfillment, the filling full, of perception.

The way of the victim is lived largely in the passive voice. Ingesting, absorbing, silent suffering are his style. Only the *imperative* mood can move him from the passive to the active voice. "Stand on thy feet, Son of Man!" "Arise, go forth, for the light has come!" Forgiveness seems fundamentally involved in getting misshapen, misdirected emotions unstuck from the wrong objects that warp, wound, and destroy life, and redirected toward fulfilling objects. Only the firm demand, "Turn around and walk through that door!" can break Narcissus loose from his mirror. "Start moving, because you're all right." This peculiar feature of forgiveness—that it demands as well as declares something—must be underlined. Forgiveness *calls* for response.

The eighteenth century poet-engraver-mystic William Blake declared, "Christ inculcated one thing: forgiveness of sins. This alone is the Gospel, and this is the Life and Immortality brought to life by Jesus." "The Spirit of Jesus is continual forgiveness of Sin: he who waits to be righteous before he enters the Savior's Kingdom, the Divine body, will never enter there. . . . Forgiveness is to be accepted. . . . If the Sun and Moon should doubt, They'd immediately go out."

So for the victim revelation comes most often in the imperative, as forgiving demand and as demanding forgiveness. Only the forgiven is free to obey and thereby to respond to the demand at the heart of this special kind of pardon.

The would-be aggressor splutters in his impotence, while the actual aggressor shutters at his compulsions. Both need power—either the power to perform or the power to withhold. Revelation, then, comes for the aggressor in the *subjunctive* mood. "*If* you would let yourself be loved, *then* you would not have always to dominate." "*If* you will let your action be shaped by actualities which you now deny, *then* that bliss and peace which elude you may be experienced."

While the aesthete stands for imagination without flesh or actuality, the aggressor represents flesh, concreteness, without vision. And revelation comes to him primarily as a special kind of promise—of controlled power and of peace.

No one of us is either purely aesthete, victim, or aggressor. These are simply nouns or names for elements that operate in all of us all of the time. For some the human problem is principally lack of knowledge to guide imagination; for others it is primarily lack of love, including self-affirmation; for others it is primarily lack of peace and self-control. But if we suffer from one of these needs dominantly, the others plague us recessively. Every part of us needs healing. The whole of our lives transpires in some measure of darkness and frightening silence. So that the Light which breaks forth, the Word which addresses us, is "precategoreal" and "trans-categoreal." It comes in many modes and among them as disclosure, as demand, and as promise.

The Core Characteristics of Revelation

I trust that we have established the "multimodal" character of revelation and that it exceeds any one-to-one relation to human powers when it encounters man. While we have been underlining the fact that revelation comes in many forms, wears many faces, and has many sides, we have yet to explore what revelation is in itself. Has it certain features that are present no matter in which form it appears?

The answer is, "Of course," but with this fundamental qualification. Revelation is marked by certain surprising characteristics for which most of us are naturally unprepared. Before we begin our characterization, however, we must make the same kind of basic observation as before: the three features of revelation that we shall examine are not its only features nor are all three invariably present every time it appears. They are primary elements, however, and so often attend revelation that to miss them may result in missing God's action itself.

The first of these features, for example, is that revelation is *apocalyptic*. Apocalypse is associated with shattering, violent eruption—with that which puts an end to the present world. Light *breaks* forth. Revelation *bursts* in. It does not simply fulfill our natural expectations. Revelation overwhelms. It kills in order to make alive.

In ancient Jewish apocalyptic there *had* to be a Day of Yahweh, a Day of Wrath, when sun and moon and stars are darkened, when the heavens are rolled together and the earth is shaken—there must be destruction—before Yahweh can become the Deliverer of the faithful and the moon shines and the sun and the sun's light is increased sevenfold. Deserts and waste lands become fertile and beautiful and men live in joy and gladness. Destruction must precede deliverance, a point echoed in Eliot's famous line: "In order to grow well / the sickness must grow worse." Our present world must come to an end.

Revelation is usually apocalyptic. Thus while it brings knowledge it is not of the kind we would *naturally* expect. Not "Grow up," but "Except ye become as little children." Not "Get a little more," but "Give much more; all that you have." It breaks in, not as propositionally stated fact, but as personally imaged embodiment, a portrayed person. Not as a simple extension of our already existing knowledge but as an ingressive archetypal event that shatters and rearranges all our knowledge. There is a paradox here: Without some preparation for revelation there would be no recognition of it when it comes, but once it is recognized it reverses virtually all of our preparatory expectations.

In Truman Capote's *Other Voices, Other Rooms,* Zoo—her real name is Missouri—urges: "Good Lord don't care whether you *smart* er not. Don't nobody but white trash ker that. Lord only kers whether you got it." The "it" is that knowledge not altogether of this world, that knowing that requires *imaging, envisaging*—aesthetic strengths—and leads to becoming. Only by the destruction of our typical conventional knowing is our imagination delivered; transformed for this *real* knowing. I recall the reaction of a friend upon first going to the Museum of Modern Art and seeing an exhibition of Jackson Pollock's painting. He came reeling out of the Museum and exclaimed, "God, I've never seen red before." I chided him, "Come on, you've seen red all your life." He explained that there had been something about the strange juxtaposition and arrangement of the colors that did not simply add something to his already existing store of knowledge, knowledge of color. These paintings had gotten hold of his eyes and his perceptual equipment and actually altered the very way he looked at the world. "I will never again look at red through the same eyes in the same way," he declared. Not only had something come *in* from the outside and enlarged him: something had gotten inside him and actually transformed his whole outlook on the world.

A second surprising feature of revelation is its *corporate character*. At a time when our national tradition still overestimates the power of the single individual and romanticizes "the solitary 'I,' " we must be reminded of revelation's history and context. It created a new Israel. It comes to men together. Joel Knox, the young hero of that same Capote novel, sees that you either go forward together or you go around in circles. So he tries to walk a plank thrown across the swampy, festering stream.

Starting over, he felt he would never reach the other side: always he would be balanced here, suspended between land, and in the dark and alone. Then, feeling the board shake as *she* started across he remembered that he had someone to be together with . . . and he could go on.

Revelation is eminently personal, but it comes to him, as R. W. B. Lewis insisted, who can be a companion: sharing another's pain, sharing with another his bread. Revelation dawns in symposium—that drinking and talking together. Companionship and symposium, bread and wine, breaking and pouring out. Camus knew this much about meaning. In *The Rebel,* after a teasing and torturous exploration of redemption in secular terms, he asks: "What good is the salvation of one if all are not saved?" He moves toward the fact of human solidarity. And in *The Plague,* Rambert, who had his chance to flee Oran, is asked why, at the last moment, he stayed: "I concluded that it would be shameful to try being happy by oneself." Companionship, symposium, and sharing solidarity require a special sensitivity, a capacity for suffering, a special kind of loving, which in their purity are strengths of the victim. Revelation seems to seek and await a corporate context for its breaking forth.

A third characteristic of revelation is that it presents itself in a distinctive pattern and yields itself only to those who seek to reenact this distinctive shape. It comes as action. Another colleague, Professor Stephen Crites, once noted this in a memorable sermon. Jacob wanted to know God's name, he recalled. But the Unnameable disclosed itself only when Jacob wrestled with him. And the Unnameable reveals his identity to Jacob by giving *him* a name in the midst of the struggle. Jacob has to recapitulate the angel's movements and *then* he comes to know the identity of the angel ("One from the Lord") *and* his own identity as Israel (lit. "He who strives with the Lord").

In Jesus of Nazareth, a man in all his humanity gets killed, but is strangely made alive again. Could it be that the meaning of that riddle—which we surely want to fathom—is given only to those who are also willing to die? "Except a seed die and fall into the ground..." Except you let that old passion for domination, for power over, for control, be crucified, you cannot be raised into a new kind of life.

Mimesis, or imitation, was the secret of Greek education. Learning by repeating. I sometimes attend ethnic music dance recitals, displays of primitive patterns. The audience is small and often sits at leg level on the floor. We are encouraged, as soon as we perceive the patterns—which are simple, stylized, and repetitious—to stand up and join the dance. Only when we are participating in the dance ourselves, we are told, can we really find it, feel it, know it. Jesus' action has a distinctive pattern: cruciform in shape, reaching from height to depth and outward to all men in every direction. It comes as action. Only when we join *this* dance ourselves can we really know it.

We clearly do not receive revelation simply through perception, through acknowledging it, but by a kind of remembering which leads us to reenact the very riddle whose meaning is then alone disclosed. Revelation has to be experienced in the form through which it is expressed if it is to be understood. St. Irenaeus talked about salvation through recapitulation. That's what revelation demands. Since it is in the active voice, it requires an active response

—a *mimesis* of the divine pattern which extends from heaven to earth and outward to embrace all men.

Where Does Revelation Occur?

Granted that revelation comes in many forms and is most often apocalyptic, communal, and response-demanding, *where* does this light break forth? Professor Tillich suggests "everywhere."

There is no reality, thing, or event which cannot become a bearer of revelation. . . . There is no difference between a stone and a person in their potentiality of becoming bearers of revelation. . . . Ocean and stars, plants and animals, human bodies and souls are natural mediums: the movements of the sky, the change of day and night, growth and decay, birth and death, natural catastrophes, psychosomatic experiences—illness, sex and danger—all these natural phenomena and all these events *may* be bearers of revelation.

That *may* be, but the witness of classical Christian faith is that for the light to be recognized everywhere it must first be seen somewhere. Though many-sided and not exhausted by our categories, it has a character: it is not "any old thing." Although it fulfills the self, revelation meets us as another. And the preëminent place it breaks forth is in the person of Jesus of Nazareth. "Human beings only seem to decide concerning the truth about life in general when they are confronted by *a* life in particular," wisely writes Van A. Harvey.

But by insisting that revelation breaks through primarily in history, we have raised at least three fundamental problems. One is that of even getting to this person Jesus in historical terms. When he is sought in history, a number of earlier critics thought, Jesus remains—in objective terms—"unknown, unnamed and lost," and yet immediately, rather mystically, *experienced.* Contemporary scholars are a little more optimistic about finding the historical Jesus. They deny both his *utter* inaccessibility *and* his immediate, altogether mystical, presence. Hard scholarship, they insist, can provide us a core of genuine teaching and practice that, while not exhausting the person, does exhibit him. Technically speaking, then, the historical Jesus is sufficiently knowable for the inquirer to confront in him the question: "Is he the disclosure of God's intention for human life?" Enough is known to see that he stands for and points to God. *Enough* light breaks through.

But, the second problem, even if one can find him in history, even if light once shone, wasn't that two thousand anguish-filled years ago?

We seem to have one of two convictions about the past. The first is that, even if the events that compose it be found, it bears little relevance to the present. We may dismiss it jocundly, like Henry Ford's "History is bunk," or we may mourn its passing in Truman Capote's words: "Was, said the weeds, Gone, said the sky, Dead, said the woods, but the full laments of history were left to the Whippoorwill." With either mood we declare that past events have little shaping role in the present. And we proceed, coping through a kind of willful forgetting, deprived of memories of a lost home country or the hope of a promised land.

An alternative conviction is that the past keeps living in the present. Indeed, psychoanalysis contends that this is an undeniable fact. If the past is unrecognized, it may produce problems. "What makes old age hard to bear," remarked Somerset Maugham, "is not the failing of one's faculties—physical or mental—but the reality and burden of one's memories." If, on the other hand, the past is remembered and acknowledged, that recollection can heal. Every time the Jewish community meets for worship, it recalls who it is. Israel is Israel only because it has its history as a people. For better or for worse, national character *now* has grown from the events of *then*. I am who I am only because I have a living past. Certain patterns, once perceived, keep reappearing. Although it first happened once back then, it is not all gone. We may remember and lament, remember and celebrate, or remember and renew our covenants. But all remembering, whether painful or pleasant, heightens self-understanding.

Capote's Zoo once more has an apposite word: "There's lots you don't know . . . All kinds of strange things . . . mostly they happened before we were born: that makes them seem to me *so much more real*." This second conviction—that the past keeps living in the present, that things long ago are real because they shape things now—is a key basis of Christian faith, which thus requires a special kind of remembering. "For without the fact [and

pattern] of the past," declares Robert Penn
Warren, "we cannot find the present or dream
the future."

Even if one starts, however, with the assumption that history—past history—shapes
the present and if inquired into, is accessible,
he swiftly comes to see that its significance for
the present requires determining what it meant
then *and* interpreting what it means now.
Things change. And this is our third problem.

If Jesus of Nazareth were the preëminent
event of revelation back then, how did they—
his interpreters—understand him? And more
important, how shall we understand him, since
until we do we shall not fully fathom how he
shapes our present?

That is the task of the next chapter. Before
proceeding, let's attempt a summary of the
main points of this one.

Calvin suggested that a study of human
frailty moves us to contemplation of God. Our
study underlined men's need to have, and to
do, and to be. Aesthetes lack the first, victims
the second, aggressors the third. Revelation,
God's light, comes as disclosure in the indicative, granting us perception. It comes as demand in the imperative, granting us pardon. It

comes as promise in the subjunctive, granting us power for control as well as power to perform. With perception we possess. With pardon we can act. With power we can be.

Revelation is often not understood because of three of its surprising characteristics. Apocalypse is associated with it. It may have a destructive as well as a delivering side. It may lay us low before it raises us up. Revelation also seeks a corporate context. It addresses us individually but only as we are in or claimed by community. And revelation requires that it be reenacted if it is to be received at all.

The preëminent place where this light breaks forth is Jesus of Nazareth, who can be encountered adequately enough by historical study but who cannot be understood unless one is willing to stand under at least three requirements: to imagine, to share, to reenact what is given. These responses are not *altogether* foreign to the ways by means of which we already cope today. There is some contact. The same faculties are used, but in a radically transformed way.

Their transformation is inextricably bound up with the work of Jesus of Nazareth, to which we now turn.

III

Whom Do Men
Say That I Am?

In spite of the sometimes inconsistent, apparently fragmentary, and uncertain character of the New Testament record, the central elements in the life of Jesus are clear: He leaves home as a young man, is baptized by John the Baptist, conducts a ministry in Galilee, consorts with the outcasts of his society, preaches and acts in a distinctive way, and is crucified. For those who believed in him, this was not the end. Jesus lived on for them with the authority of supreme victory.

These early believers, in their desire to interpret this man for themselves and for others, ascribed three major titles to him. Since the Jewish believers had recognized him as Messiah, which means literally "the anointed one," early Christians used the names of the three classes of "anointed ones" in ancient Israel as interpretive titles for Jesus. Some stressed his role as Prophet, indicating that his disclosures met the great human need for perception. Others stressed his role as Priest, underlining that his redemption granted needed pardon. Still others understood him as the King whose power is paradoxically expressed through his suffering, which empowers by eliciting power.

Prophet

Jesus apparently never hesitated to use this particular designation for himself and from the outset his followers recognized that he stood in that great line of Hebrew prophets. It was the office of prophets to speak for God and he, prophetically, "taught them as one having authority."

The initial function of the prophet was to enlarge his hearers' understanding of God, and this Jesus certainly did. It is striking, however, that his method consisted of combining and transforming individual elements or teachings they already knew into a pattern that, thus drawn together, seemed new. From their knowledge of books like Hosea and from their training and worship in the Psalms, his Jewish hearers knew that God was long-suffering and merciful. Yet when they perceived that this particular Messenger, Jesus, was himself that Message, they understood anew the depths of the divine mercy: that God cared about man and his world to the extent of taking the initiative himself to suffer and to heal it. The world's waywardness and man's moral unrectitude had threatened the very balance of creation, and in Jesus believers saw God offering himself to repair that warpedness: God righting things. Luther and the other Reformers centuries later picked up a central point of St. Paul's, that no man doubts that there is *some* ultimate power. The burning question is, What is that power like? Is it malevolent, demonic, bent on the destruction of man? Or is it beneficent, merciful, and good? As prophet, Jesus disclosed that the ultimate power is loving and just, and yet that it is a tough love, containing in it hatred for that which destroys the beloved. Jesus' primary disclosure about God, then, is that He is infinitely merciful and yet unswervingly just.

This prophet, through word and deed, also insists that God is concerned for the transformation of the world, not for the abandonment of it. If iconography in both classical pre-

Christian religions as well as the eastern religions be any clue, the question that exercised those religious minds—once the idea of divine creation had in some form entered their traditions—was whether deity, seeing that the world is now flawed, was going to turn away from it and abandon it, or was going to stick with it and try to put it back on the track. They painted that question, so to speak, on their vases and religious objects. They sculpted that question mark. And that grave question surely bothered the sensitive Jew of Jesus' day. Has Jehovah become so disgusted with the world's misuse of its endowed freedom that He is now going to turn away? Has mankind, has Israel, so broken and shattered itself through its waywardness and infidelity that Jehovah judges it now drained of all value and intends to abandon it? As prophet, Jesus reveals God's decision to stick with his world and his unsurpassable effort to hold it together and put it back on the ontological and moral track again. The continued waywardness of the world may appall the believer, but after this kind of living identification by God with the world, its worthfulness can never again be absolutely doubted.

But Jesus' most vivid disclosure about God,

perhaps, is that God himself "compassionates," suffers with mankind. Jesus reveals a God who himself struggles against the forces of disruption, who personally pays the terrible costs of restoring the world and maintaining it in being. Jesus reveals a God who has so intimately invested himself in this world that when Jesus suffers, God suffers. Luke refers to Jesus' growing up, which is always in some measure painful, with the single verse: "Jesus increased in wisdom and in stature . . ." The Greek word here for "increase" means literally to be extended by blows as a smith stretches metal with a hammer. That means that, in Jesus, God himself knows the hammer blows of human existence. God himself suffers with his world. That was Jesus' preëminent disclosure about the nature of God.

Karl Barth maintains that in his disclosures about God, Jesus the Prophet serves as a window. As we carefully examine his career, it suddenly becomes transparent, like a clear glass, and we see through it directly into the heart of God himself. On other occasions, that life suddenly becomes a mirror, and in examining it we strangely find ourselves being revealed to us. This latter emphasis is crucially important, for this particular prophet was bent on disclosing understandings of realities other than God himself.

He laid bare, for example, the need of nature and society for redemption, as well as individual man's need for salvation. God's special investment of himself in Jesus was clearly a submission of himself to the processes of nature. To be embodied means inescapably and at the least to be composed of molecules and amino acids. Our references in the first chapter to the jungle of chaotic disorder at the level of subatomic particles, and our references now to changing life processes, were efforts to underline that Chance often seems regnant in nature. Those hideous anomalies of animal and plant life (mongoloid children, two-headed calves, birth-injured man and beast), avalanches and typhoons, sores and suffering all testify to the capacity for waywardness built into and spasmodically exercised by nature. St. Paul urged that Sin and Death were the two final enemies which God had to overcome. But Jesus reveals that a third, Chance, is as ultimate a challenge. Chance, let run wild, would produce far more chaos than we presently see and would finally run itself down into *stasis,* a final static equilibrium, which *is* Death. Nature, too, needs taming, redeeming, persuasion to remain maximally lawful. An early Christian theologian, Athanasius, in another theological context once declared: "What God does not assume is not redeemed. What God does assume needs redemption and is redeemed." Jesus the Prophet *is* God's "assumption" of physical nature. In him the need of nature for redemption is highlighted. The active presence, as Tillich puts it, of "a structure of the demonic" in nature is fully disclosed. Jesus' triumph over Sin, Chance, and Death, however, symbolically reverses nature's otherwise unchecked downward tendency to deathful uniformity and reveals the power of God to bring victory out of the worst that nature, shot through with chance, can produce. Jesus reveals how deeply "nature, also, mourns for a lost good," but how God's wrestling with it prevents its deterioration into random, final destructiveness.

This prophet also disclosed society's need for redemption. The synagogue of his day, like the church in ours, was the symbol par excellence of the Establishment. In breaking it open, Jesus revealed the potentially devouring, life-suffocating power of institutions that no longer form life, but stunt and repress it. He exhibits the demonic potentiality of every social institution and the need of every social institution constantly for reform. His overwhelming revelation of God's character and intention actually initiates that social reformation.

And, of course, by being what man ought to be, this prophet revealed the depth of our plight, us individuals who are what we ought not to be. Simply by being a solid, honest, faithful man, he shines a searchlight which discloses the demonic depths of our pride, overwhelmingly demonstrating that pride brings suffering to innocent people as well as being finally self-destructive. Pascal put this prophetic insight with his usual pungency: "The knowledge of God without that of man's misery causes pride. The knowledge of man's misery without that of God causes despair. The knowledge of Jesus Christ constitutes the middle course, because in him we find both God and our misery."

Echoing Barth, then, we want to stress Jesus' "windowing" function, revealing as prophet the very nature of God; and Jesus' "mirroring" function, revealing the need of nature, society and individual men for redemption. But as prophet, Jesus discloses one more central reality that we simply must recognize: the source of possible new life. This might be called the prophet's function as "model."

He constantly calls for entrance into God's Kingdom, but always couples this challenge with the proviso, "Except ye become as little children . . ." He is certainly not calling for regression into childishness, as scholars and preachers have long pointed out. He is calling for childlikeness, for that special kind of realism and sharp clarity that children (before we conventionalize them with our training) characteristically display. He is demanding that childlike capacity for the ruthless acceptance of fact as fact ("Look, Mummie, the Emperor has no clothes on!"). In our case, childlikeness means unqualified acceptance of the fact that our lives are being ravaged by the poison of pride, which perverts our perspectives and leads us into all kinds of self-deceptions. We are sick and we need a savior.

Very little that this prophet *said* was, in itself, new. His life was his declaration. What he does is his word and he is what he does. In this respect he clearly stands in the prophetic tradition of Israel, for prophets in the Old Testament (Jeremiah, Hosea, Amos, e.g.) not only testified through perceptive words but through embodying acts. They enacted their message. Similarly Jesus' distinctive sayings gain their power, as Professor Ernst Fuchs has pointed out, not so much from their originality as from the fact that they are commentaries on already performed action. He says what he has already done. And it is the conjunction of word with deed that makes Jesus' work as prophet so telling. He does not make his disclosures primarily in pronouncements or in propositions, but in person. What a prophet!

Priest

In ancient religions, Jewish and otherwise, the priest always used something besides himself for sacrifice. But just as the first Christian believers saw in Jesus a prophet like no other —a Messenger who was himself his Message, fulfilling that role with a kind of finality—they saw him as a priest like no other—one who offers himself, his own person, as the sacrifice. Sacerdotal sacrifice was supposed to redeem, to save. *Salus,* the ancient root for "salvation," means literally "health." To be saved means to be restored to health, and this is what the priest's ministrations were deemed to do.

In calling Jesus High Priest, the early Christians were stressing that his sacrificial action pardoned and produced healing where there had been no health. But how?

As priest, Jesus opened up to those around him the possibility of a new, whole life by bringing to birth a new goal within them, quickening their desire for it, and profoundly altering their relationship to the source of strength for realizing that goal. Plato once declared that "Our souls take on the character of that to which they give themselves." Augustine echoes Plato: "A man is what he loves." Luther makes the same point: "A man is what he worships." Hawthorne's homely parable, "The Great Stone Face," says it too. The young Yankee Ernest stares so steadily at the great stone face that in time his own features reflect and have taken on the shape of those in the great face. As priest, then, Jesus initially provides his own person as a goal, a model of fidelity, that moves some to desire that kind of life for themselves, a set of new relationships.

And as they enter into a new relationship they themselves become different.

As priest, Jesus also mediates the power for transforming their lives. Commenting on the dynamics of healing, doctors note the necessity of three elements: the availability of whole-making power, some effective mediator between the patient and it, and the quickening of the patient's willingness to appropriate the power. We profoundly need healing, being made whole, as Jesus' prophetic ministry revealed. Our wills and emotions need to be made one with our intellects, so that we desire the appropriate things, have the power to realize them, and come to some measure of understanding of the entire process. Most of us, however, are inwardly fragmented, at war with ourselves, needing personal integration. And this particular priest offers to us, as to those who first recognized his priestly office, a living connection with whole-making power. He offers to mediate it, God Himself, to us. And that living offer generates in many a desire to get well and a movement in that direction. This priestly action, to be sure, does not exempt us from further evil and the continued corruption of periodic, excessive self-preoccupation. But it does supply us the power to begin moving in the direction of health.

The manner in which this particular priest performs his function is as strikingly unexpected and surprising as was his prophetic style. Sacerdotalism is usually connected with liturgy and ritual. The priest pronounces holy words, a sacred formula, which come through time to be taken as efficacious. Jesus, to be sure, *said* things which were fundamentally a part of his healing, priestly ministry. But instead of relying on talk or complicated articulated prescriptions, his characteristic priestly move was taking his place beside the person in need as one would at the bedside of a sick friend. Patients of Freud, reports Hilda Doolittle, initially rebelled because he sat where he could not be seen and sometimes said nothing for four or five sessions. Embarrassed by the silence, feeling abandoned by him, the patients railed out at Freud and filled the room with curses, protests, and lamentations. Finally, sensing the doctor's presence, although he still had not spoken, they began to hear themselves and the senselessness of so much they said. Their problems fell into perspective. By withholding talk Freud was able to serve as a hearer, a mirror. And people were healed by this silence, because it was full of personal presence. It contained judgment, to be sure. But it also contained salvation, health. This kind of priestly action is far from those rituals in which the participant, though exactly as he was before, is now treated as if he were something different. In this kind of action, the participant is himself transformed. So the priestly work of Jesus combines healing action with speech to transform the sick of soul.

The King

In many ways this final title used by the early Christians for Jesus is the most profound. His career had revealed to them just how completely—and how irreparably from their side —the bridge was out between themselves and God. And yet in Jesus they saw God himself suffering with them in the heart of their plight and restoring himself the relationship between himself and them. "God alone/can atone." He builds back the bridge between himself and man. Jesus' kingship, they insisted, is triumphant and glorious, and yet, rather than being merely a legacy from birth, it is achieved through suffering.

Let's look at the three great attempts made by the Church through the ages to indicate how Jesus, as King, "atoned" through his suffering, restored man to his proper role by providing him desperately needed power, and is disclosed as triumphant Lord. Two basic principles must guide our thinking about any doctrine of the atonement. First, no theory can be acceptable that compromises God's character as good or splits the activity and disposition of Jesus—as if God were a kind of reluctant potentate demanding appeasement and Jesus a pleading advocate for the world's forgiveness and restoration. "God was *in* Christ" was St. Paul's contention, and surely he was right.

No theory, furthermore, can be an acceptable treatment of atonement which suggests that guilt can be transferred from one person (or mankind) to another, even if that other is Jesus. An innocent person cannot become guilty by fiat nor can a guilty person, by some magic, suddenly become not guilty. A theory of scapegoat won't work. Real redemption must be far more radical than a simple transference of spiritual status.

With those two conditions firmly in mind, we can examine far more readily a first great attempt at expounding the meaning of atonement, one associated with that remarkable and much too busy Bishop of Rome at the end of the sixth century, Gregory the Great. Scholars have called it "the ransom theory," for it is clearly informed by one of Gregory's principal tasks as Bishop, literally buying back Christian citizens of Rome who had been captured by various pagan tribal chieftains. It must have occurred to Gregory one day that God buys back captive man from the Devil, using Jesus —the King incognito—as ransom. Gregory vividly characterizes that moment in Hell when Satan, gloating over having added the just-dead Jesus to his collection of captive souls, suddenly discovers to his pain and dismay that Jesus is not dead but is alive and is a cosmic champion who promptly defeats the Devil and his associates and takes all the formerly imprisoned souls back to glory with himself. This "harrowing of hell," a notion which remained immensely popular right through the middle ages, was one of Gregory's prime images for how atonement works. His other favorite image was borrowed from a fourth century predecessor, Gregory of Nyssa, but was reinforced by his knowledge of fishing, a major industry of his day with which he was well acquainted. The Roman Gregory embellished the image as Robert L. Calhoun reports: "In one of his sermons Gregory uses the ancient image of the Devil as the chaotic power, the great fish (Tiamat), the one who is and resides in the abyss. He describes how God uses Jesus the Lord as a bait, so that when the Devil snapped at that apparently human figure he was caught upon his divine power and was thereby himself taken captive."

Gregory's conceptions are obviously crude in a variety of ways and contradict both of our requirements for an adequate doctrine of atonement. The notion of God's making deals with the Devil is thoroughly repugnant, and all the more so since the divine triumph depends completely on deception. God's offering of Jesus as payment clearly splits the activity of deity. Despite these overwhelming defects, however, the direction or intention of Gregory's conceptions has elements of truth that simply must not be abandoned. After all, man does need to be liberated from the powers of evil. We are enslaved to evil. And only a kind of harrying of our hell can relieve us. This cannot be done by trickery or force, crudely conceived. Only light, entering the gloomy depths, can dispel the deep darkness in which we are enshrouded. Only love, living in the midst of hatred, can purify and break the bands of that hate. That love *is* a new power. And Gregory, in his best moments, sought to understand "ransoming" in this inner sense of indwelling illumination, an element we should surely preserve in any, perhaps synthetic, understanding of the atonement.

The second great attempt at framing an atonement doctrine was made by the late-medieval philosopher-theologian, Peter Abailard, in reaction to those elements of Gregory's thought that had been preserved and extended by Abailard's contemporary, Anselm. (This was Anselm of Laon, who echoed the doctrine of the much greater Anselm of Canterbury.) Abailard found abhorrent the suggestions that the Devil had a claim on man and that God did business with Satan. He found equally objectionable Anselm's special suggestion that Jesus' redeeming work somehow transformed the attitude and heart of God. God does not need propitiating. Man needs altering. "Actually," says Abailard, "God has always forgiven, long before the coming of Jesus Christ, which surely shows that God's forgiveness does not depend on his propitiation." The atonement thus has to do, not with wringing some change in God, but with the transformation of man. How?

As he worked in his study Abailard noticed those large moths, bearing tiny vermin on their backs, that passed through the flame of his candle and had those ugly foreign particles burned away without themselves being consumed. Maybe, he conjectured, that is a parable of what happens to man in the presence of Jesus' Cross. Like the moth, man is drawn irresistibly to the purifying light of Jesus' example. He passes back and forth through it, by study, worship, and reflection. And slowly his life is altered. The vermin of his sin are slowly burned away. And all this occurs inwardly. Or just as flame can kindle a flame in certain material brought close enough to it, so man, when he draws near the figure of Jesus, has just such a transforming flame kindled in him.

Although historians rather unfortunately chose to call Abailard's doctrine "the moral influence theory" because of its stress on atonement's being primarily human change instead of divine alteration, they were not altogether beside the point. For Abailard's view clearly underplays God's special action in Jesus and overstresses the subjective shifts within men. Although this is its weakness, it contains—as did Gregory's—some indispensable elements. Atonement must include this kind of inner quickening, again in Calhoun's words, "an awakening in man of new springs of activity, a change in man's fundamental direction and disposition." And Abailard's emphasis upon the Suffering King as model is one that any sound doctrine must retain.

Anselm of Canterbury completely worked out during this same period a third great understanding of atonement, labeled "the satisfaction theory," against which in particular Abailard had been reacting. Anselm's theory reflected the common practice in medieval Teutonic society of one family or tribe indemnifying ("making satisfaction" to) another family or tribe for crimes committed against it by some member of the first group. Family or tribal holdings were contiguous in those times, and if a member of my family transgressed the line and committed an offense against a member of another group on his land, only the providing of satisfaction to the offended group by another member of my family—or perhaps my entire family—could rectify things and settle the blood feud between us. So it is between man and God, reasoned Anselm.

Though earth and heaven are contiguous, man has repeatedly crossed the line and offended God by claiming rights and powers belonging solely to God. There is now a blood feud between man and his Maker. Only the offering of himself as a sacrifice to God by an innocent member of the family of man can heal the breach and make satisfaction. Jesus is mankind's representative.

As it stands Anselm's theory also violates both our basic principles. It splits Jesus from God and understands God as one for whom, to quote Calhoun again, "the substitution of an adequate recompense will serve as well as the punishment of the one who is actually guilty." If, however, the theory could be fundamentally altered so that it declared it was God himself who was present in Jesus' action, then it would illumine a most important point about the moral structure of the universe and provide a most helpful insight into the meaning of atonement.

The strength of "the satisfaction theory" is

its stress on the need for the *relationship* between God and man to be altered. The forgiver
has to undergo change as well as the forgiven.
To let the framework of right be violated with
impunity would destroy the ground for any understanding of goodness and justice. Since it
has clearly been violated, some kind of "making right" has to be done. Man, needing forgiveness, clearly does not have the resources
for such an objective rectification. God, on the
other hand, since he is good, cannot simply
annul the past, indulge the evil, and casually
"mark things off." Since he alone is capable, he
himself has to perform the alteration. As the
forgiver he has inwardly to bear the sorrow,
pain, and burden of forgiving. As man must
undergo change, so God too has to wring out a
painful inner alteration through his own sacrifice. And this he does in Jesus, the King whose
crown is a ring of thorns.

Our initial question about this king's suffering, you recall, was: How does it empower and
transform man? What does it mean to say that
the King's suffering "atones"? With the aid of
the sound elements from these three great
atonement theories we are now in a position to
offer some answer. Jesus' kingly action is like

79

a light shining in the darkness, which illumines our situation and liberates us. (Ransom.) It elicits inner quickening, like fire kindling fire. (Moral Influence.) It is nothing less than God himself taking the initiative and by his action altering the relationship between us. (Satisfaction.) As King, Jesus embodies the limits to which Goodness will go in order to bring men simultaneously to themselves and to it and that is why divine kingship has always been paradoxically associated with suffering.

Those early believers claimed that this kingly action empowered. They knew, however, that this power can't be external, presented or pumped in from the outside. It had to be awakened in their depths in order to transform those depths. The old pieces of their fractured inner lives had to be rearranged in fresh new patterns. The broken circuits had to be rejoined so that the power always potentially there, but lost, could finally flow. And that, they claimed, is precisely what the Jesus' kingly action does. In popular legend, kings know only pomp, glory, and heights. This king knows the depths—despair, utter alienation, Hell—and in emerging victor over them is truly worthy of being hailed "King of kings and Lord of lords." He is triumphant over all challenges.

To summarize this chapter: Jesus of Nazareth was deemed by his followers and by the Church since to have met those three great needs of the self: for perception, for pardon, and for power. As Prophet he revealed a host of things—about God, the world, society, and themselves—as much in deed as in word, and so met the great need for perception. As Priest, he made whole by connecting men with the source of forgiveness, and so met the great need for pardon. As King he suffers and restores a right relationship between man and God—rejoining broken circuits, replacing destroyed bridges, healing breaches—and so triumphantly provides the power desperately needed by men.

From the outset the question for his followers was: What manner of man *is* this? Man, god, demi-god? By the fifth century the Church had chosen a formula which has, in some fashion, been normative ever since. We must explore it in our next chapter before confronting, in the final one, the meaning of all of this for us today.

IV

From Chalcedon
to Chicago

Ernst Troeltsch, as well as other observers, has pointed out that every social group, however free of structure it may begin, eventually institutionalizes itself if it persists through time. The Christian church was certainly no exception. From the outset it began developing patterns of worship, so that the community every time it assembled could, through relatively fixed forms of prayer, exposition, and reflection, remember who it was and thus be renewed. It developed an ethic, a way of life, which it urged upon converts as being appropriate for "the children of God" who followed Jesus. And, of course, the Church developed theologies and creeds, attempts to set forth (for all time, many of their formulators thought) the basic elements of Christian belief. "Christology," the effort of thoughtful believers to declare who and what Jesus was and what his relationship to God was, exercised the Church to an extraordinary degree, especially in the early centuries of its life. It seemed that describing Jesus' work—as prophetic, priestly, kingly—was considerably easier than explaining his person.

In 451 A.D., however, at the Council of Chalcedon in Asia Minor, the largest ecumenical council of antiquity framed a formula that has had a normative effect in the Church ever since. Unfortunately, the doctrine declared there was stated in language already sufficiently ambiguous and dated to prompt immediate controversy, which has continued—wherever the matter is seriously discussed—right down to today. The council declared of Jesus:

. . . We all . . . define that there is to be confessed one self-same Son our Lord Jesus Christ, perfect in godhead and perfect in manhood, truly God and truly man . . . of one being with the Father . . . and of one being with us . . . the peculiarity of each nature preserved and concurring in this one person . . . not divided or separated into two persons.

If standing in the classical Christian tradition binds one to an understanding of Jesus somehow like this formulation, how can we, in this year of our Lord, possibly understand and accept it? Furthermore, how can it positively illumine our understanding of the preëminent revelation of God in Jesus? And how can it actually shape and contribute to our style of life in this present world? These are the questions we must explore in this chapter.

As with our reflections about doctrines of atonement, so here, in our efforts to understand ancient Christology, we must avoid from the outset a common misunderstanding. There was not—as some popular accounts might suggest—a simple escalation of the incredible in the early Church, as if the first unusual claim for Jesus was his miraculous conception, then his mighty miracles, then his corporeal resurrection, culminating after several centuries in the claim that he was "truly God." The sequence of these assertions was very different. They are not all of the same order. The key to them all is the experience by Jesus' followers of the resurrection, and that highly mysterious event is clearly related to the transformation wrought in their lives by Jesus, even after the crucifixion. So early Christians did not claim that Jesus was divine and genuinely unique *because* they already believed in a host of things we now find incredible. Rather, they subsequently framed stories of his miraculous birth and mighty works in the effort to amplify their already existing conviction that he was divine, in this sense "truly God." These stories are really retrospective evaluations growing out of his effect on their lives that they symbolized by resurrection. And that fact—the transformation of human life by Jesus—still remains finally the only ultimate basis for asserting his divinity.

Truly Man

Scholars have noted that the prime intellectual difficulty for the majority of would-be Christian believers in our century is exactly the reverse of the problem for those in the early centuries of this era. We have trouble understanding how a fully human Jesus could have been divine. Influenced by Hellenistic philosophical categories, and being pious men, many early Christian thinkers could not understand how a divine lord could be human. How could the infinite become finite? How could the eternal become temporal? How could the perfect become imperfect? Locked in this dilemma, a number of these thinkers advanced theories, the final effect of which was to declare that Jesus was God and only appeared to be a man (which is to say, he was not fully human). The history of Christian thought has been, in many ways, the history of a fight against softening this paradox: truly God/truly man.

Two brief examples from the early period of Christian history may illustrate this tendency toward denying Jesus' humanity. A late fourth century theologian, Appolinaris of Laodicea, advanced the intriguing idea that while Jesus had a physical body like ours (*soma*), and even a "personality," an animating or sensitive "soul" like ours (*psyche*), his mind or rational principle (*nous*) was none other than the mind of God himself (the divine *logos*). This is surely a lofty conception, but since in those days the mind was considered to be the ultimate center of personal life, Apollinaris's Jesus simply did not have a human center. And since it is this center of our lives, from which everything we think and do issues, that needs to be redeemed, his Jesus does not identify with us at the point of our deepest need. It was against Apollinaris's idea that Athanasius uttered his famous dictum noted in our last chapter: "What God does not assume is not redeemed."

Monophysitism was another such heresy from this same period. Its proponents claimed that Jesus' body presented the outward shell of a single man, but that behind that shell Jesus —rather than being actually individuated as we are—possessed a "universal, abstract human nature, a generalized humanity." He was then not finally a particular individual man, but mankind incarnate. While the efforts of the Monophysites to make Jesus universal are commendable, they obviously did so at the expense of his humanity, finally making him non-human.

As difficult as the doctrine of Chalcedon is, it is obviously attempting to defeat just these kinds of compromise. Whatever else Jesus is, they are declaring, he is fully human. He is "truly man." The Church has always struggled to maintain this truth, especially in periods of puritanism when flesh and bodily functions are thought somehow unworthy, demeaning, and finally undesirable. Against this denigration of the flesh and as a reminder of Jesus' full humanity, Professor Emil Brunner eloquently writes:

He was a "weak" human being like ourselves, who had to eat and drink, who got tired, so also he was a man who had to submit to the will of God, and who had to struggle, "in all points tempted like as we are," a man whom we see asking God, listening to God, praying to God, thanking God, one who was neither omnipotent nor omniscient. He could tremble and faint, and plead with God to remove from him the bitter cup of suffering. He was a man who lived as a Jew in the late period of the ancient world; who shared the views of his time, and expressed himself in the language of his people.

Being fully human, Jesus of Nazareth is limited in his understanding of his world. He can and does err, making mistakes in judgment. He believed literally in demons, for example. Everyone of his era did. It is important to remind ourselves through him that mistakes and sin are not synonymous and that sin-mastery does not require omniscience! Jesus was, as another early theologian, Origen, put it: "First the wailing infant, then a growing boy, and only then the man."

The nineteenth century Russian writer Turgenev, as quoted in J. S. Whale's *Christian Doctrine,* beautifully captures this point:

Once we were all standing waiting in a church when a man came up from behind and stood beside me. I did not turn towards him, but I felt the man was Christ. Emotion, curiosity, awe overmastered me. I made an effort and looked at my neighbor. A face like everyone's; a face like all men's faces. The eyes were looking straight ahead; the lips closed, not compressed; the upper lip as it were resting on the other; a small beard parted in two; the hands folded and still; and the clothes on him like everyone's, and most disappointing, mud all over his boots. "What sort of Christ is this?" I thought; "such an ordinary, ordinary man. It cannot be." I turned away; but I had hardly turned my eyes from this ordinary man when I felt with unshakeable conviction that this *was* Christ standing beside me. Suddenly my heart sank; only then I realized that just such a face—like all men's faces—is the face of Christ, and just such feet— boots with real mud on them—are his.

Ordinary men periodically pass through the hell of self-doubt and despair. In his exposition of that article in the Apostles' Creed which says, ". . . He descended into Hell," John Calvin insists that Jesus' Hell was in large measure precisely this sense of self-doubt and despair, of alienation and abandonment, that ordinary men experience. "My God, my God, why hast thou forsaken me?" Jesus cries out. He has been faithful to his mission, as best he understood it, and yet, after less than three years in it, he is hanging here on a cross. Had he misunderstood the whole thing? "Why hast thou forsaken me?" To be human, Calvin urges, is to experience these anguishing depths. Jesus was truly one of us, for the phrase, "he descended into Hell" means no less than that he, too, knows the depths of abandonment, the abyss of despair.

One persistent, unfortunately phrased claim of the Church for Jesus has consistently threatened to undo this clear conviction that Jesus was fully human, namely, the claim that he is "sinless." Abailard, who greatly helped us in our understanding of atonement, provides us with an anatomy of sin that may prove equally clarifying. The first stage toward sin, he suggests, is simple temptation (*temptatio*), the envisaging of waywardness or moral error. Temptation is always accompanied simultaneously by a second stage, delectation (*delectatio*), the pleasureable excitation accompanying the envisaging of waywardness. However, insists Abailard, there has thus far been no sin, for being human means to be lured by the possibility of wickedness and to be titillated by the prospect. Sin occurs only when the will takes the next, or third, step, consenting (*consentio*), or yielding to the temptation. And the fourth stage is simply enactment (*actio*) of the tempting design. Because Jesus was human, Abailard declares he constantly experienced those first two stages: ". . . in all points tempted like as we are." Yet in every instance, after what must have been the most fearsome struggle, he chose not to yield but to remain on the track. He knows the power of temptation as clamorously as any man, but he continually exhibits the "power of a higher affection." He is committed to a task. At any moment he could abandon it and turn aside. There must have been many moments when the temptation to do just that was enormous. But he remains faithful. So that Jesus' accomplishment should be labeled "sin-mastery," and not mentioned with that picayune privitive term "sinlessness." We should not ever suggest that Jesus' overcoming of sin and finishing as its master was because he was, a priori, divine. To the contrary, he proves himself divine precisely because he does not yield to sin. "Like as we are . . ." This ancient anatomy of temptation and choice is purely apropos today. So much of the human dilemma consists of struggling to determine which voices should be answered, which urges honored, which places entered. This fact virtually dissolves the complaint that "I just can't *identify* with Jesus!" He hears the siren sounds, he contemplates short cuts and "get-it-quick" schemes—the temptation stories in the Gospels are efforts to underline it. He struggles. And so do we. That's what it means to be a man. Like us in this regard, he was "truly man."

Truly God

Two cautionary words must precede our examination of this other side of the Chalcedonian paradox. First, we must be aware that even the holders of the very highest Christologies never made the simplistic, crude assertion: "Jesus is God," as if the two were absolutely identical, exhausted into each other, as if God's habitat during Jesus' lifetime were confined to Jesus' body! Theologians *have* contended that Jesus' nature was of "one essence" or "of the same substance" with God's.

But they have preferred phrases like "Son of God" or "God's self-objectification" in characterizing Jesus. They were attempting to say, I think, that the *quality* of Jesus' life is of the same quality as God's life, and is, in this special and qualified sense, of one piece with it. Jesus *participates* uniquely in God's life. We must avoid suggesting that, in Jesus, God has "come to earth" completely, without remainder, as has been suggested recently by Professor Thomas J. J. Altizer, a leader of "the death of God" school of theologians. God invests himself in his creation and preëminently in Jesus, but nature and Jesus remain under God's judgment, as well as under his loving superintendence. He is distinct and distinguishable from them. He is not exhausted by them or identical with them. Altizer's is a cheap way of glorifying nature or earth.

Thinking in simple quantitative terms is the other conceptual pitfall we must avoid. If we say that Jesus is "fully human" and "fully divine," we may be confronted with an insoluble mathematical puzzle. People have sometimes roughhewnly reasoned that Jesus' selfhood was like a pitcher. Once it is poured full of humanity, it is simply impossible to pour it full again of divinity. No pitcher can contain twice what it was created to hold! A much better formulation of the doctrine would obviously be "fully (a quantitative term) human/truly (a qualitative term) divine." And that, insists Calvin, is just what the church at Chalcedon was trying to say, that this fully human man, Jesus of Nazareth, nevertheless exhibited a quality of life that was truly divine.

Now we can see that the phrase "truly God" does not assert that in Jesus all of deity has entered human existence *completely*. It is declaring that, within the limits of human existence, deity has broken through *truly*.

Judaism and Christianity have both understood God in terms of love, truth, wisdom, and power. The whole of the divine power and wisdom are obviously not present in Jesus. These are, after all, divisible features: one can possess more or less wisdom, more or less power. And Jesus seems to possess no more wisdom or power than any of earth's best men. Love and truth, on the other hand, are not divisible. One is not more or less loving, more or less truthful. One either loves and has love, or he doesn't. One is either truthful, or he isn't. Power and wisdom are susceptible to

94

quantitative analysis. Love and truth are not. And the Christian claim is that while God's wisdom and power are not completely present in Jesus, God's love and truth are, in unalloyed fashion. This presence of the divine love and truth in the person of Jesus answers the haunting question of Luther that we noted in the last chapter: What is the *nature* of that mysterious ultimate power whose reality no man can doubt? Were it only omniscient we ignorant men would cringe. Were it only omnipotent we would cower. But the love and truth of God purely present in Jesus convince us that the divine power and wisdom are loving and truthful. Origen again offers a telling summary image characterized in Robert Calhoun's lecture notes:

Suppose, he says, there were a statue so immense that the eye of man could not take it all in at one look. Obviously the best way of conveying to man the lineaments of that statue would be to present man with a small copy of it in which all the features would be represented on exact, smaller scale. And this is what God has done in Jesus. He has made himself intelligible by offering us a miniature of his own being. He shows us what he himself is like within the bounds of finiteness.

The love and truth of God purely present in Jesus reveal to us the nature of the wisdom and power of God not completely present in him. Jesus brings God into human focus.

The startling fact that is revealed by Jesus' life and its divine quality is that God himself suffers. Suffering is not foreign to the divine nature. To be divine is to suffer. The unusual work of the New York psychiatrist, Dr. John Rosen, may furnish us a parable of how the free, but personally costly, identification by a healer with one in need may redeem. Conventional psychotherapy, as you know, is practiced with people sometimes paradoxically called "normal neurotics," i.e., people whose disturbances are not so deep or overwhelming that they have lost their powers of speech. Conventional psychotherapy depends on the exchange of words. But patients with deep psychoses often slip into catatonia, through long stretches of which they live in apparently impenetrable silence. How can the psychiatrist reach them? How can he rouse them even to the level where conventional psychotherapy can begin?

For the period during which he is going to work with a group of these most deeply disturbed patients, Dr. Rosen moves in on their ward, placing his bed right alongside theirs. On the initial morning having addressed a patient with "Good morning," and having received no response ("Surely he is aware," whisper the knowing nurses, "that that man hasn't spoken in ten years!"), Rosen suddenly strips off his coat, tie, and shirt and climbs directly into bed with the patient. He then begins the most intimate kind of mothering and loving. He loves and embraces the patient again and again, wordlessly, employing only this primitive language of gesture. He follows the same procedure a second, third, fourth day, sometimes for weeks, conveying to the patient in the most fundamental, altogether preverbal language man possesses, the language of gesture, that he *is* loved. And slowly, after varying periods of time, many patients are loved back into speech. Their first words are often a halting "Thank you."

It is as if God initially used the Law and the Prophets, conventional methods, in the attempt to restore the world. But our sickness was so severe that nothing short of God's moving in on the ward with us and confronting us directly could begin the healing process. And this he does in Jesus, whose "technique" is not so much that of speech but of action. In his action, through his gestures, doubt about God's nature is dissolved. God is suffering love in person. This is the clue to the claim "truly God."

Questions, Hints, and Guesses

We have no illusions about having fathomed the divine mystery through our exposition or about having dissolved the paradox of Chalcedon. "God comprehended is not God." But hopefully the intentions of the Church in framing its ancient doctrine about Jesus are clearer and we are able more intelligibly to decide whether they were correct.

This claim, "fully human/truly divine," has always raised at least three questions. Let's conclude this chapter by examining them.

First, "If, by having this divine quality of life, Jesus is in some measure different from other men, is that difference merely one of degree—his having *more* love and truth than we do—or is it a difference in kind?" Those nineteenth century philosophers of process or becoming help us here. They noted many realities that, if one began adding to them in degree, broke over at some unpredictable, critical point and became different in kind. In one sense Jesus exhibits only more love and truth than other men, but because they are altogether unalloyed, what might be called a mere difference in degree is a difference in kind.

Second, "Is Jesus the only revelation of God?" Of course not. But the classical Christian claim is that he is an indispensable and decisive one. Recall from our second chapter Professor Tillich's emphasis on revelation's being potentially found everywhere. Our contention is simply that, in order to be found everywhere, God must first be found somewhere. "God, who in former times spoke in various ways to the fathers through the law and prophets," speaks finally in a son. In that son people recognize things about God, their world, their society, and themselves that they had not seen in that depth before. They concluded that in this son, Jesus, God was doing what they, as pious Jews, had been awaiting. And so, beginning there—"in Jerusalem and Judea"—they were able to recognize God everywhere, "unto the uttermost parts of the earth." So it is today. If I first seek God "everywhere"—in nature or in myself, for example—I find very indistinct and sometimes contradictory clues. When searched for signs of God, nature often seems to testify as much to the diabolical as to the divine. And when I look within myself in search of God I often find only the reflection of my own face, seen as at the bottom of a deep well. When I first find God in the historical person of Jesus, however, I can return to nature, armed with my understanding, and find in it supplementary testimony. I can look at myself in the light of my understanding of God initially drawn from elsewhere, and find within corroboratory witness to him.

Third, "Could there be another Christ, another one of whom we would be constrained to declare, 'truly man/truly God'?" In principle all things are possible. But a second or third can never be a first. And why would we desire or require a second or third if all we needed were bodied forth in the first? Historical events cannot repeat themselves, and the classical Christian claim has been that in Jesus history turned a corner and that his life has shaped and qualified everything that has come after it.

But has Jesus—Prophet, Priest, and King, fully human yet truly divine—really changed world history and individual life? If one replies, "Yes," as I should certainly want to do, the question then becomes: *How* can my history, my world, and my life be altered through this person, this revelation?

The prevailing Christian answer has been, "Through appropriating this revelation for yourself." Each epoch in the Christian era has had its own understanding of primary human needs and has, therefore, suggested its own method of appropriation. St. Paul, for example, thought that men needed to "imitate" Jesus' life—"Let this same mind be in you which was also in Christ Jesus"—and so he urged them to grow in faith, hope, and love, principal elements in Jesus.

Each of the sixteenth century Reformation schools had its own understanding of human need and the corresponding life-style that would be an answer to it. In Calvin's view man's primary need was for knowledge of God, and he proposed the gaining of this knowledge through obedience. For Luther, man's greatest need was for reconciliation with a righteous God, and he urged reconciliation through that ancient, but redefined, virtue, faith. The Anabaptists and the Free Spirits—Hans Denck,

Sebastian Franck, Schwenckfeld, Castellio, and the others—insisted that "kingdom citizenship," life in a community of the redeemed, was the greatest human need and that it could be met through participation and discernment.

I mention these various prescriptions in order to underline the propriety, indeed, the necessity for each generation to determine, in the light of divine revelation, its greatest needs. And if God's revelation in Jesus is lasting, as I am convinced it is, it should prove suggestive of the most appropriate life-style for our generation, as I believe it does.

In summary, then, and in preparation: We have examined our human needs in general: the need for perception, pardon, and power. We have looked at the natural ways we attempt to meet these needs, with little or no reference to revelation. We have carefully explored the nature of revelation and particularly its content in the classical Christian understanding. We now have to review our situation in the most concrete, practical terms to determine whether we can appropriate "God in Christ" for our situation. If we could, what style, what "way of coping"—and overcoming —would come forth?

V

The Way of the Pilgrim

The world in which we live, as depicted by the contemporary American novelists mentioned in the first chapter, and as reflected in their own titles, is "lonely," "strange," "hollow," and "alien." The hero, or antihero, in these books—who, after all, is supposed to illumine *our* condition—is, as Franklin L. Baumer noted, "shipwrecked," "thirsty," beset by "disease." "And in the sacred history of *this* man on earth," comments Ignazio Silone, "it is still and always, alas, Good Friday."

You will recall that Ihab Hassan helped us isolate five elements composing this world of current American fiction. As these artists see it, this is the nature of *our* world, the "natural" world. It is marred by (1) absurdity—*absurdus,* which in Latin means harsh or grating, and at its root, *surdus,* means deaf. R. W. B. Lewis writes: "Our world is a tuneless world, a tone-deaf world," which is often perceived,

Jean-Paul Sartre suggests, like a giant TV set with the volume turned off. Its second feature is (2) utter normlessness, where all gestures and events have equal weight. Lighting a cigarette, catching a bus are as important or unimportant as God, murder, sex, a career. They are all equally valuable or valueless. (3) "Hell," Sartre again wrote, "is other people." I cannot achieve community with them and because I can't, they forever threaten. So the third feature of life-in-the-world is inescapable alienation. (4) Every action, furthermore, is beset by ambiguity. "Self intrudes itself," says Reinhold Niebuhr, "every time thought gives way to action." (5) Finally, partiality and limitation—a profound relativism —marks all our thinking and doing.

I have been suggesting throughout these chapters that this is an accurate diagnosis of our dilemma when appraised without reference to revelation. But I have also been insisting that there is available a power for adequately and appropriately coping with the world, a power which also alters our estimate of it. In the second chapter we characterized revelation, the power in question, as apocalyptic, coming in the midst of and creating communities, and demanding its reenactment in order to be received.

Now, if the natural world is as the artists portray it—absurd, normless, alienated, ambiguous, and thoroughly relativized—and if revelation nevertheless breaks into it, how ought we to respond to revelation in this kind of world?

We spoke generally in the second chapter about the need for imagination, sharing, and a capacity for *mimesis* or recapitulation. We must now speak concretely.

There is a fourth way or style that reflects life being transformed. It retains the strengths of the ways of the aesthete, the victim, and the aggressor, but it puts them into a new framework. The primitive pattern of *this* way is the dance. Its fundamental gesture is the embrace. And its archetypal figure is Immanuel, God himself with us, who is actualized in Jesus. This is the Way of the Pilgrim. Let's see concretely how the way of the pilgrim alters our situation.

The World Turned Inside Out

(1) The only way order is realizable in an absurd world, the only way saving sound can

break the sinister silence, is through love. Our Capote hero, young Joel Knox, senses this: "There was no prayer in Joel's mind; rather, nothing a net of words could capture, for, with one exception, all his prayers of the past had been simple concrete requests: God, give me a bicycle, a knife with seven blades, a box of oil paints. How could you say something so indefinite, so meaningless as: God, let me be loved."

We've long known that only he who is loved, and can allow himself to be loved, can himself love. Only the beloved can be a lover.

In the life of Jesus of Nazareth we have the demonstration of God's love for us. But only through reaching out—imaging that love, sharing it, living it—can we be remade by it and pass from knowing *about* it to knowing it. When we know God's love we are free to love him *and* our neighbors.

The surest test of whether we've grasped and been grasped by divine love is the extent to which we reenact it. Thus Nora Melody chides her daughter, Sara, in O'Neill's "A Touch of the Poet": "O it's little you know of love and you never will, for there's the same divil of pride in you that's in him and it'll kape you from ivir givin' all of yourself, and that's what love is. It's when you don't give a thought for all the 'ifs' and 'want-tos' in the world." Love is complete, unqualified self-expenditure. The psychoanalyst, Harry Stack Sullivan, puts it in clinical terms: "Love is that interpersonal relation where another's security and satisfaction are as important to me as my own." Only when we recognize that we've been loved like that—by God, in Christ—can we truly love ourselves and *then* "do we know that we are passing from darkness into light, because we love the brethren." Again it is our knowing that God loves us that allows us to love him, our neighbors, and ourselves. It is this certainty that "he first loved us" which frees us to make "the securities and satisfactions" of our friends as important as our own to us.

(2) Once *one* event, one in the past that constantly breaks forth into the present, becomes the cornerstone of our lives, we are no longer normless. But how can we know (a verb we've frequently used) with any certainty which anchoring event to choose? The fact of the matter is that we cannot *know* beforehand —with anything approaching absolute certainty—that the cornerstone we are choosing

is the normative, the key one. At some point one has to dare, to gamble. The issue is "when?" and "how?": at first blush, or after some sound preliminary weighing? It is against those who prematurely and impetuously leap, in the throes of panic on first seeing their plight, that Nietzsche's excoriation cuts: "O you weary after-worldly who want to reach the ultimate with one early leap, one fatal leap: weary with yourselves you want no more—so you create gods and afterworlds and then leap, o leap, to them." Nietzsche's is a salutary warning against precipitate leaping. But we do eventually have to risk, to gamble, sometime, if only after carefully scrutinizing the half-dozen or so key events or images that have the power to serve as norms. The Christ event—crucifixion and resurrection, midnight and dawn, defeat and victory, death and life—offers itself as just such a normative event. One is not called upon to leap into it upon first inspection, but after a while we come to terms with it either by embracing or by consciously rejecting it. And it may be, in some strange way, that after embracing it conceptually one discovers that he had long since himself been embraced by the actuality whose "truth for

108

him" he is only now acknowledging cognitively.

The kind of certainty we seek comes only afterward and may be a different kind of certainty from that which we had expected, one in which conceptual problems still remain but to be grappled with now within a new sense of support. Francis Fergusson has described the "movement of the tragic form." It begins with a *purpose* (do something about the Theban plague; revenge the killing of the former king) that moves through *passion* (action, conflict, suffering) and then is followed by *perception* (the wisdom begotten of pursuing the purpose passionately). So it is with the sequence of embracing a norm. It is not altogether unlike the work of creative artists who, if Dorothy Sayers' analysis is correct, thrash around in the midst of unshaped, impressionistic experience, then seek to *express* it, and only then *fully* recognize what it is they experienced. This sequence—where that peculiar kind of not altogether conceptual certainty comes a posteriori —suggests that we first engage the potentially normative event of God in Christ through that special imaginative remembering, recollection. Pondering its shape and substance for a pe-

riod we finally either reject it or begin reenact-
ing it. And the testimony of those for whom it
has become the cornerstone of existence is that
recognition follows the reenactment. The Word
speaks only after a long silence and to those
who, sensing its nearness, step out, gambling
on its support.

(3) Involvement is clearly the answer to
alienation, that third mark of our dilemma.
Most of us remain more suspended than involved, I suspect, like Richard in Christopher
Fry's "The Dark Is Light Enough," of whom
the Countess observes:

> Richard sometimes reminds me of an unhappy
> Gentleman, who comes to the shore
> Of a January sea, heroically
> Strips to swim, and then seems powerless
> To advance or retire, either to take the shock
> Of the water or to immerse himself again
> In his warm clothes, and so stands cursing
> The sea, the air, the season, anything
> Except himself, as blue as a plucked goose.
> It would be very well if he would one day
> Plunge, or dress himself again.

I really cannot say enough about the im-
portance and necessity of involvement in the
world with which Jesus wrestled and on behalf

of needy men for whom he gave his life. It does require compassion, "suffering with," and if one has that, "acts of mercy"—to use Biblical language—must follow. Involvement is urgent. As the young hero of Reynolds Price's *A Generous Man* says: "I have learned my lesson . . . that the worst thing of all is not paying your debts—and paying in time; you got to give people what they need *in time,* not years too late when they've famished and fell."

But here a cautionary word is in order. Overwhelmed by human need, sickened by the Church's becoming a closed ark of salvation, a cruise ship with only the right kind of people on board, and disgusted by the preoccupation of religious people with their own souls, prophets have arisen today challenging us to junk transcendence and to plunge solely into the world of needy men. But as we respond, there is the danger of forgetting that it is God—who, to be sure, is always found with my neighbor—with whom we have ultimately to do. In fact, according to George F. MacLeod, the greatest human temptation always has been to dismember the Cross by denying its horizontal beam, the reaching out to all men in every direction. But in our time there is the other danger, dismembering the Cross by denying its vertical beam, to settle for a humanism which denies theism. But "it is thou, O God, in whom alone to abide is to stand firm," declares Augustine. "Thou alone who dost fortify. If Thou shouldest be lost, all would come to nothing."

The Cross is the conjunction of God with man. It does not pit them against each other. And if we feel alienated, becoming involved— "rejoicing with those who rejoice and weeping with those who weep"—is the antidote, but always so that hope does not get swallowed up by love, so that prayer does not vanish in the white heat of action or become a brisk, mechanical recital of formulae to pep us up and improve our action. "And remember," says Evgraf in *Doctor Zhivago*, "you must *never*, under any circumstances, *ultimately* despair. To hope and to act, these are our duties and misfortune. To do nothing and finally to despair is to neglect our duty."

Jesus Christ reveals the nature and scope of our alienation. It is from God, neighbor, and self. But Jesus sets forth a way that alienation is overcome, through involvement that springs from communion with God. We're in for a long haul with those social problems that most concern us now and a special stamina and renewing is going to be required of us. Prospero's old observation is so presently apropos: "And my ending *is* despair, unless I be relieved by prayer."

(4) Ambiguity, that fourth feature of our life in the world, is bound to mark every action. But it much more fearfully flaws those actions that spring from a static center than those that flow from a source that is itself constantly being transformed. If one is, as Paul Greene urges, "forever growing," forever being renewed through growth, then one's action is likely to be riddled with less ambiguity. His action then comes from a center that has stayed abreast. Ambiguity most marks intentions that have to travel dark, cavernous distances before ever becoming actualized, or actions in a changing world that come from a center that doesn't change.

Faulkner's Portia Beauchamp quaintly chides us all: "Us talk and act like our own Mama and her peoples and their peoples before them. You have to think out everything in your brain. While us rather talk from something in our hearts that has been there for a long time. And act when our growin' heart just swells."

The only way to have that growing heart—which is not cold—and that heart that through its growing is near the light and not buried in darkness, is for a constant transformation of the heart to be going on. Light, bringing warmth and illumination, must be continually breaking in, nullifying—keeping at bay—the powers of darkness. It's to men in whom such transformation is taking place that Augustine can say, "Love God, and do whatever you will." Ambiguity is never finally overcome. It is a constituent of being human. But the paralyzing guilt that mounts with our awareness of the way ambiguity tinctures everything can be attenuated. One can be graced to move on in full awareness of the ambiguity, which is certainly part of what "growth in grace" means.

(5) Most of us seek to outrun relativism, that fifth feature of our situation, through mobility or versatility. We think that if we scramble fast enough up the inclined plane toward success, we can escape the parochializing features of relativism. Or, if we'll master enough skills—scientific experimentation, folk singing, a good game of golf or badminton, daz-

zling conversation on most anything most everywhere—we can triumph over partiality. We try, and there grows a sense of failure. We cannot transcend our birth-decreed, background-given limitations.

Spontaneity, the capacity to respond freshly and appropriately in each new situation, is the only antidote that can seriously minimize the pinch of relativism. It must be a shared spontaneity and it must be, paradoxically put, habitual spontaneity. Habit as such suggests being frozen in a fixed position. I am urging, in contrast, learning how always to be spontaneous. Musical improvisation is a clear example. Only the musician who has practiced and is thoroughly disciplined is able to improvise. He has mastered his medium to the point of becoming able to be free within it. Improvisation at the keyboard by one who had never touched a piano would produce inept grating. Improvisation in the dance by one who had never danced before would be a grotesque joke. One has to be in shape. Repetition is initially involved in learning to be spontaneous, but it seeks to be repetition without rigidity. It is demanded of us from others and comes to full flower with others.

Habitual, shared spontaneity is the only way of authentically narrowing the relativity gap. If our judgments are wooden, encapsulated in concrete systems, they are bound to betray a pitiful partiality. But if they spring forth fresh, each one an appropriate response to the environing situation *in that moment,* then many of the negativizing features of our inescapable relativism can be minimized. It was this emphasis that led William Blake to insist that righteousness in the New Testament was—and had to be—an instinct: "Jesus was all virtue and acted from *impulse,* not from rules. He did not ponder." He proceeded, as N. O. Brown agrees, "a graceful artist or dancer who would ruin the dance if he had to pause or stopped to figure out 'the relevant bases' of the next step." He was full of grace—and truth—and invites us who have not joined at the piping, to rise and dance.

One must take thought, but there is a kind of habituation of the vital wellsprings of our personality, so that they hear that music the world often misses and respond to its tune.

Self-consciousness about one's limitations is paralyzing, crippling. Spontaneity is freedom, the freedom to move.

116

Jesus of Nazareth *is* the apocalyptic, community-seeking, recapitulation-demanding revelation that has entered our world. In Chapter 2 we used the metaphor of the dance, noting the way in which guests at ethnic music recitals are often urged to become *participant*-observers. We stressed then that primitive dance always has a pattern, its distinctive "content," if you will. The two succeeding chapters have sketched the content of the Christian dance. It is cruciform in shape. It requires moving in the direction of love, choosing a cornerstone or key reference-point, becoming involved with God and man, learning always to grow, seeking spontaneity. These responses, which represent examined spontaneity, turn our absurd, normless, alienated, ambiguous, relativized world inside out. Such is the dance we are invited to join.

To Be A Pilgrim

A form of living in which these elements are present leads one into "the way of the pilgrim," the person who moves, cares, and is engaged. If I had to speak in a single phrase of this style, composed of these several elements, I would call it "self-expending, self-fulfilling forthgoing," or—in less barbarous language—"commitment to radical vocation."

Radical vocation is a special possibility in our post-bourgeois period. Never have people, students especially, had so open a chance for shucking The System and really living. This surely is the secret of the power of the contemporary literature we've mentioned, which portrays men in extreme situations—in the midst of death, abandonment, despair. For it is only in extreme situations that a man's whole powers—all of them—come into play. *In extremis* one really lives. And so radical vocation, which calls one down and out to the extremes, offers the real possibility for life. Those deficiencies of having, doing, and being that plagued the aesthete, victim, and aggressor are fulfilled here in a way that involves each of their strengths—imagination, sensitivity, boldness of action.

In its most extreme form radical vocation means literally giving oneself away, like that twenty-eight year old priest, the brother of a friend of mine, who was killed three years ago in the January 16 Pakistan riots while helping some Hindus who were under assault. It means an expenditure of oneself beyond the limits of law and rationality, in a kind of uncalculated self-surrender, a divine intoxication more sober than sobriety itself. It means transcending those crippling cocktail-party comments of friends, "It's a pity he's deserted good sense for some social bee in his bonnet." Shucking the system is not easy, nor can it ever be done completely. But it is a challenge and a goal—living free from the tyranny of "they"; liberated for the community of "we."

The fundamental gesture of the pilgrim's way is the embrace—loved by God and loving Him, moved by men and loving them. Through soaring, absorbing, or assaulting—flight, capitulation, capture—the aesthete, the victim, and the aggressor sought *control,* as if freedom were found in some kind of domination. The pilgrim does not seek control, but *focus.* Freedom, we are contending, is found at the intersection of God with man, the transcendent with the human, the ultimate with the most intimate. The problem is focusing on this intersection and bringing one's life into focus. Caring for others, which embrace symbolizes, also involves renunciation. There is a time for actually embracing and a time to refrain from embracing (Ecclesiastes 3:5) but all time is determined by caring, by the love which embrace signifies.

In the Cross love and death, caring and renunciation, giving and going are gathered. And the pilgrim finds focus through embracing the reality in the Cross. Wherever ultimacy is thus united with intimacy the word becomes flesh, and the flesh can become word-filled without denying itself.

One's loneliness becomes communion with others without contamination. And communion becomes community without exile.

Professor Vincent Harding reports a moving spiritual sung by Odetta, "He Had A Long Chain On." The song grows out of the antebellum practice of binding three slaves together for auction along a single chain. At the outset of the song, one man, obviously the middle man, shows up alone at the house of a lady, bearing that long chain. He seems to have gotten partially free. She's frightened by his request for food, but finally has him come in, chain and all, and serves him. After a while she suspects that this may be Christ—". . . inasmuch as ye did it unto one of the least of these . . ." She looks into those sad, wise eyes and says, "Can't I free you? Can't I knock that chain off?" But he replies, "You just let that be," and leaves humming a tune like "Come with me." He had a long chain on.

This is the Christian declaration and invitation. "Join me. Take my yoke upon you." In joining the divine chain gang that stretches around the world, one is freed from every tyranny. Not hoarding, but spending oneself. Not protecting one's meager privacy, but pouring oneself out. Not isolation, but communion with all. These realities are united in embrace.

"Radical vocation," "self-expending, self-fulfilling forthgoing": the classical name for this style is *"imitatio Christi,"* the imitation of the archetype, Christ. But it really is, if I understand Christian faith, an *"imitatio dei,"* an imitation of God himself. The contemporary theologian, Arthur McGill, puts it clearly:

The otherwise difficult idea of the trinity—God's triunity—grows out of references in the New Testament to what is called "the Father" and "the only Son." The New Testament emphasizes that the Son is derived from the Father and depends completely on him *and* that the Son accepts this dependence and constantly offers all his own glory back to the Father. This dynamic movement continually goes on in the heart of the divine, "The Father" holding nothing back, reserving for himself no superiority; the Son, having nothing but what he receives, yet constantly receiving the entire fullness of the Father and giving it back. This means that at the heart of God we have a perpetual act of unlimited self-communication. The Father giving away, the Son giving back. So when one sees into God, he sees nothing less than perpetual self-communication and perpetual self-expenditure, the self-giving at the heart of the divine life.

Self-giving is at the heart of God's life, so in being challenged to radical vocation or forthgoing one is challenged to no less than recapitulation of the pattern of the divine life itself. "He who loses his life for my sake shall find it." "Except the seed die and fall into the ground it cannot bring forth fruit." Instead of being depleted in this self-giving we are oddly fulfilled. This fulfillment may not bear the marks of the "full life" as our *New Yorker* world judges it. And fulfillment may seem to come for some of the faithful only at the end, in death. But the life that is truly given away, like bread cast on the waters, returns at some time as new life to the giver.

In these pages we have examined man's

needs, our dilemma. We have looked at revelation that breaks forth in the midst of those needs. We have seen the special requirements involved in its reception, the way in which it fulfills our strongest faculties by radically transforming them. We have suggested that one who receives revelation has offered to him a certain style, a distinctive, sure form for personal existence—"the way of the pilgrim." His commission is to keep moving, keep loving, keep passing from darkness into light, from death into life. Life remains mysterious, indefinable, and incalculable. Evil remains dense, durable, and seemingly ineradicable. We nevertheless are constantly called to begin, to leave our hiding places and our stopping places and to commence. We are even called to dance. The late President Kennedy often closed his speeches of challenge with the ancient Chinese proverb: "A journey of a thousand miles must always begin with the first step." Our call is to begin moving. And as we warm to walking in the light, yea living in the Light, we shall surely come at sometime to that moment when with all men,—"the sons of morning"—"we shall dance and sing for joy." We shall dance in the company of God.

References

Chapter 1—Coping With Chaos

Bonhoeffer, Dietrich. *Letters and Papers From Prison*. London: SCM Press, 1959, pp. 24, 168-69.

Camus, Albert. *The Plague*. New York: Alfred A. Knopf, 1948.

Cohn, Norman. *The Pursuit of the Millenium*. Fairlawn, N.J.: Essential Books, 1957, pp. 29, 32.

Freud, Sigmund. *The Future of An Illusion*. London: Liveright, 1928.

———— *The Ego and The Id*. London: Hogarth, 1927.

———— *Civilization and Its Discontents*. London: Hogarth, 1939.

Hamilton, William. *The New Essence of Christianity*. New York: Association Press, 1961, pp. 152-58.

Hassan, Ihab. *Radical Innocence*. Princeton: Princeton University Press, 1961, pp. 116-18.

Holton, Gerald. *Christianity and Crisis*. Vol. XXVI, No. 9, May 30, 1966, p. 114.

Joyce, James. *A Portrait of the Artist as a Young Man*. (Originally published in 1916.) New York: Viking Press, 1956, pp. 183, 206, 217, 221, 238.

Kierkegaard, Sören. *Either/Or*, Part I, "A Fragment of Life." (Originally published in 1843.) Princeton: Princeton University Press, 1944.

Lewis, R. W. B. *The Picaresque Saint*. New York: J. B. Lippincott, 1959, pp. 20-21.

Mailer, Norman. *An American Dream.* New York: The Dial Press, 1965, pp. 8, 12, 31-32.

———— *Advertisements For Myself.* New York: New American Library, 1959—Signet Book T1889, p. 512.

McCullers, Carson. *The Ballad of a Sad Cafe.* New York: Houghton Mifflin, 1951, pp. 24 ff.

McGill, Arthur. *On Suffering Love.* (From lecture 3 of a mimeographed series delivered at Princeton.)

Percy, Walker. *The Moviegoer.* New York: Alfred A. Knopf, 1962, pp. 146, 194.

Poirier, Richard. *A World Elsewhere. The Place of Style in American Literature.* New York: Oxford University Press, 1966.

Styron, William. *Lie Down in Darkness.* (Originally published in 1951.) New York: Viking Press, 1957, p. 386.

Tillich, Paul. *The Courage To Be.* New Haven: Yale University Press, 1952, esp. ch. 2.

Troeltsch, Ernst. *The Social Teachings of the Christian Church.* New York: Macmillan Co., 1931, Chapter III, Parts 2 and 3.

Chapter 2—Something Present Often Missed

Blake, William. Quoted by Northrop Frye in *The Anatomy of Criticism.* Princeton: Princeton University Press, 1957, p. 66; and cited by N. O. Brown in *Love's Body.* New York: Random House, 1966.

Calvin, John. *Institutes of the Christian Religion.* (Originally published in 1559.) Philadelphia: Westminster Press, 1960. Library of Christian Classics edition, Book I, Chapter 1, #1, pp. 35-36, 36-37, 38.

Camus, Albert. *The Rebel.* (Originally published in 1951.) New York: Alfred A. Knopf, 1956.

——— *The Plague.* New York: Alfred A. Knopf, 1948, p. 188.

Capote, Truman. *Other Voices, Other Rooms.* New York: Random House, 1948—Vintage Book ed., pp. 55, 126, 179, 220.

Cohn, Norman. *The Pursuit of the Millenium.* Fairlawn, N.J.: Essential Books, 1957, p. 2.

Crites, Stephen D. "The Naming of Gods and Men," a sermon preached in the Wesleyan University Chapel, November 17, 1963.

Harvey, Van A. *The Historian and The Believer.* New York: Macmillan Co., 1966, pp. 273, 288.

Schlesinger, Arthur, Sr. *In Retrospect: The History of A Historian.* New York: Harcourt, Brace & World, 1963.

Schweitzer, Albert. *The Quest of the Historical Jesus.* (Originally published in 1906.) London: Adam and Charles Black, 1954.

Tillich, Paul. *Systematic Theology, Volume I.* Chicago: University of Chicago Press, 1951, pp. 118-19.

A further discussion by a literary critic of elements contributing to a modern understanding of revelation may be found in R. W. B. Lewis, *The Picaresque Saint.* New York: J. B. Lippincott, 1959.

Chapter 3—Whom Do Men Say That I Am?

Barth, Karl. *Dogmatics in Outline.* London: SCM Press, 1949, pp. 65-66.

——— *Church Dogmatics,* Vol. III, Part 2, #44, No. 1, "Jesus, Man for God," pp. 55-70, and #45, No. 1, "Jesus, Man for Other Men," pp. 203-21.

——— *Church Dogmatics,* Vol. IV, Part 1, #58, No. 1 and 2, "The Grace of God in Jesus Christ" and "The Being of Man in Jesus Christ," pp. 79-121.

REFERENCES

Doolittle, Hilda. *Tribute to Freud.* New York: Pantheon Books, 1956.

Fuchs, Ernst. *Studies of The Historical Jesus.* (Originally published in 1960.) London: SCM Press, 1964, esp. chs. IV, IX, X.

Tillich, Paul. *The Interpretation of History.* New York: Scribner's, 1936.

———— *The Shaking of the Foundations.* New York: Scribner's, 1948, pp. 76-78.

The threefold Christology in the second paragraph of this chapter appears in John Calvin, *Institutes of the Christian Religion,* Book II. William Hamilton has a useful section on Messianic titles in *The New Essence of Christianity.* New York. Association Press, 1966. Also helpful is George F. MacLeod, *Only One Way Left.* Edinburgh: Iona Community Press, 1956.

A further discussion of atonement may be found in Gustaf Aulén, *Christus Victor:* An Historical Study of the Three Main Types of the Idea of the Atonement. London: S.P.C.K., 1953. Also William J. Wolfe, *No Cross, No Crown.* Hamden, Conn.: Archon Books, 1962.

An elaboration of the idea of Jesus as his own Message is available in Günther Bornkamm, *Jesus of Nazareth.* New York: Harper and Row, 1960.

Chapter 4—From Chalcedon to Chicago

Brunner, Emil. *The Mediator.* (Originally published in 1927.) London: Lutterworth Press, 1934, pp. 359, 361, 363 ff.

Rosen, John N. *Direct Psychoanalytic Psychiatry.* New York: Grune & Stratton, 1962.

Troeltsch, Ernst. *The Social Teachings of the Christian Churches,* two volumes. (Originally published in 1911.) New York: Macmillan Co., 1931.

Whale, J. S. *Christian Doctrine*. Cambridge: Cambridge University Press, 1941, pp. 100-01.

Chapter 5—The Way of the Pilgrim

Altizer, Thomas J. J. *The Gospel of Christian Atheism*. Philadelphia: Westminster Press, 1966, pp. 70-75.

Baumer, Franklin L. *Religion and the Rise of Scepticism*. New York: Harcourt, Brace and Co., 1960, p. 215.

Capote, Truman. *Other Voices, Other Rooms*. New York, Random House, 1948—Vintage Book ed., pp. 73-74.

Fergusson, Francis. *The Idea of a Theater*. Princeton: Princeton University Press, 1949.

Lewis, R. W. B. *The Picaresque Saint*. New York: J. B. Lippincott, 1959, p. 61, and quoted p. 71.

MacLeod, George F. *Only One Way Left*. Edinburgh: Iona Community Press, 1956, p. 37.

McGill, Arthur. *On Suffering Love*. (From lecture 2.)

Price, Reynolds. *A Generous Man*. New York: Athaneum Publishers, 1966, p. 263.

Sartre, Jean-Paul. *Literary Essays*. (Originally published 1950-1955.) New York: Philosophical Library, 1957, p. 82.